# SPEAKING SKILLS FOR TEENS

## Create the Image You Desire

## a 14-Session Speaking Seminar

# INSTRUCTOR MANUAL

## BY GAIL A. CASSIDY

# SPEAKING SKILLS FOR TEENS

### Create the Image You Desire

### a 14-Session Speaking Seminar

## INSTRUCTOR MANUAL

## BY GAIL A. CASSIDY

**BALBOA**.PRESS
A DIVISION OF HAY HOUSE

Balboa Press books may be ordered through booksellers or by contacting:

Balboa Press
A Division of Hay House
1663 Liberty Drive
Bloomington, IN 47403
www.balboapress.com
1 (877) 407-4847

ISBN: 978-1-9822-4787-4 (sc)
ISBN: 978-1-9822-4788-1 (e)

Print information available on the last page.

Balboa Press rev. date: 07/21/2020

# DEDICATION

Tom, Lynne, and Tommy--you are my foundation, my life, my motivation. I am blessed to have your love. You will always have mine. I am additionally blessed with my wonderful daughter-in-law, Elizabeth, and two magnificent grandsons, Patrick and Jason--what a joy to have you all in my life!

To write a book requires a writer to have a strong belief in the importance of getting a particular message out to the public. My message is simple. Everyone is special in some way, and when a person is able to recognize and act on that something special, the world benefits. Mastering Communication Skills allows that to happen.

This book is dedicated to my Roselle Catholic students who helped make this book possible. I learned more from you than you ever could have learned from me. Thanks for the lessons.

# TABLE OF CONTENTS

# QUESTION??

## Can this program be used as a self-paced course?

# ANSWER:

# YES, IT CAN!!

Using this manual, anyone can proceed through each session and learn the basics of being an effective speaker and creating the image they desire.

For talks, instead of being in front of a class, stand in front of a full-length mirror, set your timer, and give your talk. The experience may be a bit more uncomfortable than you thought it would be, partially because you are not getting any non-verbal feedback from the group. As soon as you are done, self-critique your talk. The advantage you have is you can give your talk again and again until you are pleased with the results.

To present yourself with an even greater challenge, tape yourself in action and have a friend critique you, using the Critique sheet.

Be sure to read all of the background information for the instructor so you can be aware of the research dealing with body language, attitude, and the fundamentals of speaking.

Good luck in your quest to be the best that you can be. If you undertake this course on your own, please let me know how you did and what your reactions were. You can contact me at gail@coachability.com. I look forward to hearing from you.

*[Note: for ease of reading, male and female pronouns will be used interchangeably throughout the text.]*

# Dear Speaking and Imaging Instructor,

As indicated in "The Ten Worst Human Fears" list, for many people, public speaking is a fate worse than death. The good news is that no one is born a great communicator, but almost anyone can become a great communicator if they have the desire and are willing to practice. The fact is, we make presentations in one form or another every day. How we respond to questions, shake hands, talk to people are all forms of presenting. Presentation skills are worth mastering no matter what field we are in or are intending to pursue.

A study by AT&T and Stanford University found that the number one predictor of success and upward mobility is how much you enjoy public speaking and how effective you are at it. (*Training and Development Journal*)

As an educator, I was deeply moved by a story I read many years ago about Mark Edlund, a young man who lost his life in Vietnam. When his special effects were returned to his parents, they found a yellowed, crisply folded paper in his wallet. He had carried it with him since 7th grade.

That one day so many years ago, his teacher asked the class to write the names of every student in class on the left side of the paper. She then asked them to write one good thing about that person next to their name. That weekend, she took everyone's lists and made each student a copy of all of the good things their classmates had written about them. Mark Edlund had kept that paper with him all of these years as had many of his classmates who attended his funeral.

This story is significant because of the impact those words had on this young man and his classmates. These weeks will have a similar impact on your students. The reason is, at the end of the course, each student will receive all of the positive comments from fellow students about every talk he or she had given.

Compared to physics, math or Spanish, this program will indeed seem easy; however, students will learn far more than speaking skills. They will experience an entirely different outlook on life, especially regarding who is responsible for how they feel, how they act, how they react.

Students will learn to see people differently. They will learn how to "read" people and become aware of how they are "read." They will learn how to use their voice to produce the greatest effect. In other words, they will have the opportunity to mold themselves as they want to be.

While students may eventually forget facts and figures learned elsewhere, they will undoubtedly retain much of what they master in this seminar, because they will have constant opportunities to be on their feet and apply those things they have learned.

They will also have many opportunities to laugh, cry, and genuinely feel good. This seminar enables all participants an opportunity to learn "to enjoy public speaking." Why? Because everyone responds to "positives," and that is what each speaker gets from his peers and instructor--positives, what the audience and instructor liked about the speaker's talk.

On the speaker's hand-in form, the instructor will suggest <u>one</u> area for improvement sandwiched between two positives. If you use a grading system for this program, the participant's grade will depend on how well the recommendations are addressed. A "nervous nelly" has as good a chance as a polished speaker to get a good grade, because each has to address his own recommended areas of improvement.

To make the speakers as comfortable as possible, the first talks will be on topics they know well. Students will be encouraged to use a conversational tone, as if speaking one-on-one. As they become more comfortable in front of their audience, they will be encouraged to be more dynamic. By the way, being dynamic comes automatically when speakers begin to forget themselves and speak from their hearts.

The length of the sessions depends on the time available for the program. Sessions could be 3 1/2 hours each, once a week or, in a school setting, 45-minute periods five days a week. The first sessions will 1) cover procedures, 2) the basic fundamentals of speaking, 3) expectations, and 4) attitude training. To reinforce the importance of *attitude* throughout the course, you may want to post recommended quotations around the room and refer to them occasionally, especially in each session's summary period.

The curriculum for *Speaking Skills for Teens* addresses the ofttimes overlooked issue of responsibility, which is addressed through the study of *attitude, thoughts, nonverbal communication*, and an understanding of *people skills*. Participants have many opportunities to internalize the fact that while they may not be able to help what happens to them, they are in control of their reactions. That knowledge is very empowering.

Participants also learn the basics of how to create the image they wish to project. They also learn how their use of nonverbal communication impacts the perception people have of them.

The 14-week program you are about to start is one of the most rewarding, fun seminars you could ever share with people OR go through yourself as a self-paced program. As you will see as you peruse the manual, much more than speaking and imaging is covered.

Numerous benefits await the participants, but the most outstanding one is the individual validation of each participant by her peers. Let me share one testimonial from a quiet, shy young lady from one of my classes.

*"Effective Speaking is the first class that I actually truly got something out of it. There are no words to explain how I love the class so much. This is talking straight from the heart. I used to despise talking in front of the class. Now I look at it in a way to speak my mind freely. This class showed me a whole new level of confidence I never knew I had. Even though I would get nervous before I did my talks, I would get this feeling of excitement when I went to talk in front of the class. This is the first time I actually liked going to a class. This class also gave me an idea of what I want to do as a career when I get older. Not only did I learn how to talk, I learned that I am a strong, confident, and unique individual. . . . I want to thank you so much for a lesson you taught me in life.*

During her first talk, this student was barely audible. With her head bowed and her eyes on the floor, I feared I had a real challenge ahead of me. I should not have worried, however, because her peers provided her with the support and validation that buoyed her and literally transformed her into an extremely effective speaker--one who touched our hearts with her words.

For the first few weeks, approximate times for activities are included, but the actual time is dependent on the number of people you have in the seminar. The times listed after each activity are just an approximation to help you get started.

Of major importance in this seminar is the tone set by you. It can be very tempting to tell a speaker to stop fiddling in his pockets or shuffling her feet. You can take care of all the needed improvements by your comment(s) on their Planning Sheets rather than mentioning something that could cause embarrassment for the speaker in front of her peers. Writing two positive comments followed by one recommendation for improvement works beautifully. Because the speakers are guaranteed no negativity or embarrassment, they blossom. They also must know that their success depends on how well they address your recommendations for improvement.

Because you will have a card for each participant on which you write your comments, you will be able to be constantly aware of how well they have improved. A Week One fantastic speaker may still be fantastic in Week Fourteen, but if he has not addressed the recommendations, he will not have improved as he should have.

I absolutely guarantee that you will love leading this seminar. You will know at the end of the course that you have indeed made a difference, a big difference in the lives of your participants. The nice part is that you are affected as positively as are they. The transfer value of looking for positives is best illustrated by one very bright gal and terrific speaker who was in the class.

*"This course has done much more for me than I ever expected. It has not just made me a better speaker, but it has made me a better person overall. I now feel more confident in my skills to relate to other people on a daily basis. I would recommend this class to everyone because the lessons they will learn they will carry with them throughout their lives.*

*"The final and probably most important skill that I learned in class was to only look for the positive in people. Because we were instructed to write down only positive things on our evaluation cards, picking out the good in people instead of bad has become second nature to me. This skill not only makes other people feel better, but it also reflects itself on my own disposition. When a person learns to see the positive in other people it brings a much more peaceful, optimistic outlook to the rest of the world around them."*

The Instructor's Manual is formatted in a manner to make it easy for the instructor to locate not only what is happening each session but also what the necessary background material is.

The Student Manual contains a copy of every page in the Instructor's Manual which is marked "Packet" in brackets. Your copy may contain italicized material to further explain the sheet.

I highly recommend you start and end each class exactly at the time you said you would, even in a classroom environment. Participants learn to expect punctuality for the beginning and ending of class. If you start late, you penalize those who get there on time. The average class size is 25-30 people. This number provides a great deal of synergy and enthusiasm among the participants.

Each session begins with **TIPS FOR THE WEEK** (effective human relation recommendations), and each session ends with testimonials from former students. You will be told what equipment you need and what each week's objectives are. You are taken step-by-step through each session. The first few sessions are packed with background information which is easy to assimilate and remember. Interspersed among the material are appropriate, meaningful quotations from well-known people.

I hope each of you enjoys this course as much as I do.

Best wishes,
*Gail A Cassidy*

# WEEK ONE

## INTRODUCTORY TALKS

## TIPS FOR THE WEEK:

1 • See the invisible tattoo on participants' foreheads that reads:
**"PLEASE MAKE ME FEEL IMPORTANT."**
2 • Find at least one happening in each class period to be grateful for.
3 • Look for positives in every person.

### ØØØØØØØØØØ

**INSTRUCTOR NOTES:** Throughout the course, wherever you see "INSTRUCTOR NOTES," you will find research and/or background information. The first few weeks are information intensive. Once you become familiar with the information, you will be able to use it throughout the course and not just for the particular material at hand.

*Covering everything included in Weeks One and Two is virtually impossible. That is why it is important that you become conversant with the material so you can interject the information throughout the program.*

Another distinction of the INSTRUCTOR NOTES is that the text will go from the left margin to the right margin rather than be indented, which is the format used for procedures, talks, assignments, etc.

Additional bracketed notes to the instructor are found in the indented material wherever you find brackets.

## EQUIPMENT NEEDED:

- A bell to signify end of talk
- A clicker [cricket or bottle top that makes a noise] to indicate 10 seconds left in talk [or you can say "10 seconds.]
- Instructor's manual
- Participant Packets
- 5x8 cards [provided by participants]
- Name Tags (Participants wear for the first six sessions)

## WEEK ONE OBJECTIVES:

- To have participants overcome their fear of speaking in front of a group by providing them with a successful experience.
- To set a positive tone for the group.
- To introduce participants to the "Packet" in order to give them a long-range view of what to expect in this class.
- To show participants that you, the instructor, will be a part of the class by giving a sample talk for each assigned talk.
- To teach participants the importance of attitude in all aspects of life through experiential assignments, research information, and famous quotations.
- To have participants internalize that *attitude* and *responsibility* are choices they make.
- To show participants how they can control their thoughts and their attitudes.
- To have students give their first talks.

## PROCEDURE:

- Seat participants
- Take roll
- Explain that all talks are between 1 - 5 minutes                    **5 MIN.**

## ASSIGNMENTS:

- For next class, everyone bring 5 x 8 cards, one for each participant in the class, e.g., 21 participants equals 21 cards (includes one for instructor). An alternative would be for every student reserve one page in their notebooks for every student in the class.
- Have each participant print her name on top left corner of card/page on lined side <u>before class</u>.
- Cards will be used at the beginning of next week.
- For next week, their first **2-minute talk will be on Your Favorite Funny Story.** Examples: a holiday they remember, a birthday, skiing trip, visit from friend, special gift they received, doing something they should not have been doing and getting caught, an embarrassing yet funny moment, etc.          **10 MIN.**

**SAMPLE TALK:**  • Instructor gives a sample talk of how participants' talks could sound. Be sure it is two minutes long and follows the format you want the participants to follow.          **2 MIN.**

# PACKETS/INSTRUCTION:

- Distribute Student Workbooks and briefly discuss first eight pages which are as follows:

1. **Self Evaluation:** *Start in Week 2, and complete one each week.*
2. **10 Worst Human Fears**: *Discuss and get reactions from participants.*
3. **Effective Speaking Rules**: *Emphasize the importance of being themselves because that is what is special.*
4. **First Impressions:** *You only have one opportunity to make a first impression.*
5. **Planning Sheet for Presentations**: *Must be turned in for every talk unless told otherwise . Memorize opening and closing sentences.*
6. **Nervousness Tool Kit**: *Exercises from these pages will be used throughout the course.*
7. **Critique:** *Enlarged copy is posted on the wall to enable everyone to find the strength of the speaker and/or their talk.*
8. **Assignments for Course**

# ITEMS IN REMAINDER OF PACKET:

9. Presentation Fundamentals
10. Organization of Talks
11. Openings
12. Evidence
13. Closings
14. Affirmations
15. Planning Sheet for Negotiating
16. Elephant
17. Body Language Cues
18. Voice
19. Relate to Your Audience
20. Guidelines
21. Planning Sheet
22. Commitment Sheet
23. Human Relations Stack
24. Enunciation
25. Enthusiasm
26. Toward More Powerful Speech
27. Sales Presentation Planning Sheet
28. Causes/Issues
29. Persuasion Talk Planning Sheet

30. Reading
31. Final Talk

**REMINDER:** The first Planning Sheet is due next meeting.

## PROCEDURE FOR TALKS:

- Today's first talk is one minute or less. The objective is to have everyone experience a positive, comfortable speaking experience.
- Have class stand. First row faces second row; third row faces fourth row. Make sure everyone has a partner. If there is an uneven number, the instructor acts as a speaker/listener.
- Everyone who is facing the back wall will begin speaking **FOR TWO MINUTES** to her partner for two minutes, telling the listener about herself. She can discuss why she is taking the course, where she lives, goes to school, family, hobbies, whatever comes to mind.
- At the sound of the bell, partners change speakers. Those who are facing the front of the room speak next and repeats the assignment.
- At the sound of the bell, everyone sits.
- The assignment is to tell the class about the person you just met and spoke to. The person can relate anything the speaker told him.
- This is the only talk where the speaker can stand at her seat and deliver her talk.
- To get the first volunteer, ask who would like to be most relaxed for the rest of the week? Do this lightly, with humor, and surely a number of hands will go up.
- **Participants clap as each person stands. ALWAYS!**
- Make sure participants feel comfortable. Tell them the purpose of the talk is to make sure everyone knows everyone else in the class.
- Participants <u>all</u> clap when each speaker finishes. Eventually participants come to expect the applause.

**REACTION:**
- Upon completion of each talk, point out one thing you liked about the presentation, no matter how good or bad it was. [Remember, areas for improvement are written on student's planning sheet-- one specific recommendation per talk.]

- Ask the group what they liked about the presenter, the presentation, or the impact on the audience. Take one or two comments--**only positives**. Participants can get ideas from the **CRITIQUE** sheet permanently placed in front of the room. **STRESS USING THE CRITIQUE SHEET.**

DATE _____     TOPIC _____

# SELF EVALUATION

## [PACKET]

## Evaluate yourself after each talk.

RATING: (LEAST/WORST), 1 to (MOST/BEST) 10

|  | | **1 3 5 7 10** |
|---|---|---|
| 1. | Nervousness BEFORE speaking. | 1 3 5 7 10 |
| 2. | Nervousness WHILE speaking. | 1 3 5 7 10 |
| 3. | Nervousness AFTER speaking. | 1 3 5 7 10 |
| 4. | Knowledge of the topic. | 1 3 5 7 10 |
| 5. | Degree of preparation. | 1 3 5 7 10 |
| 6. | Audience interest. | 1 3 5 7 10 |
| 7. | Quality of voice. | 1 3 5 7 10 |
| 8. | Use of body. | 1 3 5 7 10 |
| 9. | Awareness of audience. | 1 3 5 7 10 |
| 10. | Enjoyment of speaking experience. | 1 3 5 7 10 |

Make 14 copies of this page and evaluate yourself after each presentation. After your talk, hand this sheet to your instructor along with your Planning Sheet.

# PREPARE, PRACTICE, AND DELIVER!

# THE TEN WORST HUMAN FEARS
# (in the U.S.)

## [PACKET]

## 1. Speaking before a group

2. Heights

3. Insects and bugs

4. Financial problems

5. Deep water

6. Sickness

7. Death

8. Flying

9. Loneliness

10. Dogs

*David Wallechinsky, et al.: *The Book of Lists*. New York:

Wm. Morrow & Co., Inc. 1977.

# EFFECTIVE SPEAKING RULES:

*[PACKET]*

1. Be yourself.

2. Be prepared.

3. Know your audience.

4. Know the purpose of your talk.

5. Know the result you want from the audience.

6. **HAVE FUN!!!**

# FIRST IMPRESSIONS

[PACKET]

**It takes only four seconds to form an opinion. You only have one chance to make a good first impression.**

## SUGGESTIONS:

**Walk to the front of the room with your head held high and your shoulders back. Look confident and you will feel confident.**

### When you are in the front of the room to speak,

- Look out at the audience and use "soft eyes" when making eye contact for the first time. This allows the audience to "feel" your warmth.
- For formal talks, look down as you place your notes on the podium. (Podium is not needed for this class until the end, and then it is optional.)
- Talk a deep breath and feel yourself relax.
- Feel the audience's anticipation.
- Pause long enough for the audience to respond.

### Now, when they are with you, have a "knock-your-socks-off" opening sentence, and know it by heart, e.g.:

- "I'm delighted to be here . . ."
- "I understand your organization . . ."
- "On the way here today I. . ."
- "I've been asked to speak to you today about . . ."
- Three out of four people . . ."
- "The president of the United States confirmed . . ."
- "How many of you are fearful of . . ."

The exception to these recommendations is when you are giving a one-to-three-minute talk. For this class, two-minute talks should have opening sentence which answers "who," "when," "where," and "what" (notice "why" is not included). For example, "When I was five years old (when) my brother and I (who) went to New York (where) to visit my aunt (what).

**Now you can take a step toward the audience**

**Remember:**
**Know yourself. Know your material. Know your audience.**

**NOW THE AUDIENCE IS WITH YOU:**

- Speak with warmth, enthusiasm, and strength.

- Keep your face and voice congruent with your topic.

- If you enjoy yourself, the audience will enjoy you and your talk.

# REMEMBER:

# KNOW YOURSELF
# KNOW YOUR MATERIAL
# KNOW YOUR AUDIENCE

*Gail A. Cassidy*

NAME:_____ DATE: _____

# PLANNING SHEET FOR PRESENTATIONS
## *[PACKET]*

**YOUR PURPOSE IN MAKING THIS PRESENTATION:**

_____

**OPENING:** (Use exact wording) _____

_____

**POINT #1:** _____

    **EVIDENCE:**_____

_____

**POINT #2:** _____

    **EVIDENCE:** _____

_____

(you may only have one type of evidence, such as a story, for a two-minute talk)

**POINT #3:** _____

    **EVIDENCE:** _____

_____

**POINT #4:** _____

    **EVIDENCE:** _____

_____

**CLOSE:** (Use exact wording) _____

_____

**MORAL:** _____

**RESULT YOU WANT FROM AUDIENCE:**_____

# NERVOUSNESS TOOL KIT

". . . the only thing we have to fear is fear itself. . ."
-Franklin Roosevelt
*[PACKET]*

**BEFORE YOUR TALK:** Know that even professional speakers get nervous.

**Nervousness stimulates speakers to give superb performances.**

1.  **Write down why you are nervous.**

2.  **Talk to your nervousness**.

| | |
|---|---|
| *Nervous self:* | *What if I forget what I was going to say?* |
| Sane self: | You stop, look at your notes, then continue. |
| *Nervous self:* | *What if everyone notices?* |
| Sane self: | Then they notice. |

-   Everyone forgets something some time in their lives. People will understand.

-   Continue talking in your head to counter every reason you have listed for being nervous.

3.  **REPEAT A POSITIVE AFFIRMATION 3 TIMES**, e.g., "I love my topic" or

    -   "I'm totally prepared" or "I'm relaxed and confident."
    -   "This is the best speech I've ever given."
    -   "People love hearing what I have to say."
    -   "I am more and more relaxed every time I speak."

-   **BELIEVE WHAT YOU ARE SAYING TO YOURSELF.
    SAY IT EMPHATICALLY**.

4.  **Feel warmth toward your audience.** Smile and activate the feeling of joy.

*Gail A. Cassidy*

# MORE NERVOUSNESS
# TOOL KIT IDEAS:

**ABOUT TO GIVE TALK:** Remember, a certain amount of fear is good.

1. **ISOMETRICS:** Clasp your fingers together in your lap. Squeeze as hard as you can. Then relax. The tension from the exercise and the upcoming talk will dissipate. Yul Brenner, a Broadway actor who performed 10,000 performances of "The King and I" pressed up against a wall (isometric exercise) before each performance in order to release his nervousness.

2. **DIAPHRAGMATIC BREATHING:** As you are seated, take a deep breath, pushing your stomach outward. Take three deep breaths and you will find your mental clarity improved, because you will have more oxygen to your brain.

3. **QUICK RELAXATION TECHNIQUE:** After deep breaths, visualize the most relaxing scene you can think of. Visualize it in detail and feel yourself begin to relax into the scene.

4. **PHYSICAL TECHNIQUE:** In the restroom, stand tall and then let yourself bend at the waist to the floor, like a rag doll. Relax into this position and then, one vertebra at a time, slowly come back up.

5. **ATTITUDE:** Choose the attitude you want.

   - Control your thoughts, e.g., use positive affirmations.
   - Give up the idea of perfection. Being effective is about the impact your message has on audience.

**REMEMBER:** You know more about what you are going to say than anyone in the audience. **ENJOY YOURSELF!!!**

# CRITIQUE

*[PACKET]*

## PRESENTER

1.  **Posture**: poised, confident, natural, and sincere
2.  **Body language**: gestures, posture, hands, animation, open
3.  **Voice:** volume, projection, tone, variation, enunciation, effective use of pause, conversational, warm, respectful
4.  **Facial Expression**: congruent, use of eyes, use of expressions, great eye contact, warm eyes
5.  **Enthusiasm**: forceful, concise, friendly, pleasant, natural, vibrant
6.  **Appearance**: appropriate, professional, neat, groomed, polished, friendly

## PRESENTATION

7.  Catchy opening
8.  Organization of material
9.  Knowledge of subject
10. Positive feeling projected
11. Ideas clearly presented
12. Drew mental pictures
13. Clarified material
14. Avoided jargon/acronyms
15. Effective use of visuals
16. Strong closing
17. Creative
18. Effective use of questions
19. Involved audience
20. Clear purpose
21. Use of audience

## IMPACT ON AUDIENCE

22. hought-provoking, inspiring, convincing, challenging, enlightening, humorous, motivating, informative, entertaining
23. Showed awareness of audience needs
24. Sincere
25. Empathetic to audience and made them feel special
26. Conveyed emotion and excitement about subject
27. Aroused emotion in audience
28. Inspired audience
29. Called attention to audience member
30. Made a difference

*Gail A. Cassidy*

# PRESENTATION ASSIGNMENTS
## [PACKET]

**PRESENTATION #1 -** "**Introduction**" - A one-minute or less talk about class member you interviewed. You could cover the following: *Name, Home, Family, Hobbies, Job, Favorite TV shows, What they want to get out of this course*--anything you remember about your conversation.

**PRESENTATION #2 -** "**Favorite Funny Story**" - Your first **2-minute talk will be on Your Favorite Funny Story.** Examples: a holiday you remember, a special birthday, skiing trip, visit from friend, special gift you received, doing something you should not have been doing and getting caught, an embarrassing yet funny moment, etc. What did you learn as a result of this incident?

**PRESENTATION #3 -** "**Negotiating/Role Playing**" - You will be given a role to play without understanding the other persons' points of view. In small groups you will play your role and then give a **1-minute evaluation of task. 1 minute**.

**PRESENTATION #4 -** "**Favorite Person**" - Who is your favorite person and why? Tell a story about how this person became your favorite person, e.g., an encounter, an adventure, an article about, why he/she represents that is important to you. This is a **2 minute talk**.

**PRESENTATION #5 -** "**What I Know To Be True**" - 3-minute talk to inform audience about what you know to be true. **NOTICE THE ADDITION OF ONE MINUTE TO YOUR TALK.**

**Examples:** What do you know more about than most people? Are you informed about different types of music, swing dance, tennis, ham radio, hip hop, race car driving, and/or hobbies that others may not be familiar with? Use a story which includes your participation in the activity along with one other type of evidence.

**PRESENTATION # 6 -** "**Storytelling**" - Come prepared to tell a **two-minute story** and a brief appropriate joke.

**PRESENTATIONS #7 -** "**Show and Tell**" (1 minute) & "**Pet Peeve Talk**" (2 minutes) - (No preparation sheet necessary) Look for something you are particularly proud of: a trophy, an article in the paper about you or your dog or family member, a special pen you use, a special gift, an award of some sort--anything that you can use as a prop in your story next week.

- **"Annoyance Talk"** Tell about a time when something happened that really made you angry, e.g, being cut off on the highway, getting into the wrong checkout line, being falsely accused of saying something, being talked about, losing your keys, having someone borrow and not return an object, etc.

**PRESENTATION #8 - "Sales Presentation" - (2 minutes).** You will sell a product and use the outline on the Sales Presentation Preparation sheet.

**PRESENTATION #9 - "Talk to Entertain" - (2 minutes).** •You may work together for this assignment. Each participant is required to fulfill a 2-minute segment • No preparation sheet necessary • Find a play or story to tell the group.

- Notes may be used, but no reading is allowed.

**PRESENTATION #10 - "Talk to Persuade" - (4 minutes).** • Select a cause/issue you feel strongly about and persuade class to your way of thinking. • Use a variety of types of evidence (See Evidence page.) • Complete Planning Sheet indicating forms of evidence to be used.

**PRESENTATION #11 - "Reading" - (2 minutes).** • Mark your copy carefully. Refer to "Reading" sheet in your packets.

**PRESENTATION #12 - "Tips Talk" - (2 minutes).** Using the commitment you made many weeks ago, report on the outcome of applying your chosen "Be the Best That You Can Be" Tip.

**PRESENTATION #13 - Review Your Packets carefully before class.**

**Essay due last week (if applicable):** 5 paragraphs, typed, double spaced on "Of What Value Was This Course to Me?" Please construct this in the same manner you have constructed your talks. See a Planning sheet for ideas.

- Do not include a discussion of the instructor
- You may include recommendations for future changes in the course, if you desire.
- You may share your reactions about the change you noticed in a fellow classmate(s).

**PRESENTATION #14 - FINAL EXAM (5 minutes) - See instructions on your Final Examination which is in your packets.**

*Gail A. Cassidy*

# PRESENTATION "MUSTS"
## [PACKET]

1. Know your material thoroughly and have a clear focus on your topic.

2. Feel really good about your subject and **BE ENTHUSIASTIC.**

3. **REMEMBER:** The audience "mirrors" you. If you have fun presenting, your audience will have fun listening. **KNOW YOUR AUDIENCE.**

4. Create an emotional experience during talk. Lives are created by feelings, not by thoughts. Have the audience experience your passion and excitement, and they will remember your talk.

5. **Two things an audience does not forgive:**
   a. A speaker's lack of preparation (they interpret it as an insult).
   b. A negative, "I don't care" attitude projected by the speaker.

6. Effective Speaking is a skill where **PREPARATION** and **ATTITUDE** are apparent almost immediately.

7. **RECOMMENDATIONS:**
   a. Avoid dairy before speaking. It can cause mucus in throat.
   b. When of age, don't drink any alcoholic beverages ever before speaking. You could embarrass yourself if you do.
   c. Don't overeat before speaking. You may have to burp during your talk.

8. Do not memorize your talk, but to guarantee yourself a great start, memorize your opening sentence and your closing sentence.

9. **PRACTICE, PRACTICE, PRACTICE.** Rehearse in front of a mirror.

10. Visualize giving your talk. See yourself relaxed and successful.

11. Welcome a tinge of anxiety. It is a sign you will be on your toes to do the best job you possibly can do. You are in good company. Willard Scott, Diane Sawyer, plus numerous actors and broadcasters have experienced first-rate nervousness. How do you overcome it? Face the thing you fear, and fear will disappear.

12. **HINT:** Number your note cards or pages of your talk--just in case.

## 13. **EYE COMMUNICATION**:

The eyes are the windows to the soul. They communicate attitude and emotions not spoken. Eyes show your outlook on life and are a barometer of your feelings. They are the only organ in your body that cannot lie.

- Lowered eyes may mean guilt or uncertainty.
- Piercing stare can mean anger or annoyance.
- Focused, relaxed eye contact indicates confidence and reliability.

## 14. **PAUSES:**

- An effective method to get attention.
- Nothing is "louder" than silence.
- Allows the audience to focus on the speaker.

## 15. **POSITIVE ATTITUDE:**

- Felt by audience.
- Associated with energy and enthusiasm which equals credibility.
- Associated with confidence which translates to credibility.

## 16. **SMILE**

## 17. **PASSION:**

"Forget all the conventional 'rules' but one. There is one golden rule: Stick to topics you deeply care about and do not keep your passion buttoned inside your vest. An audience's biggest turn-on is the speaker's obvious enthusiasm. If you are lukewarm about the issue, forget it!" -Tom Peters

"If you can say it without passion, spare your voice and leave me a note." - Jeff Walling.

# Above all, **HAVE FUN!**

# ATTITUDE TRAINING

*Cover as much of this material as is possible throughout the course. This section is lengthy and contains quite a bit of information, which you can incorporate into sessions throughout the course. Once you are totally familiar with the material, you will be able to constantly reinforce the importance of attitude in everything participants do and particularly in their speaking opportunities.*

**EXERCISE:**
- Have five participants come up front, give each a 3x5 card, each containing one of the following words: *anger, sadness, happiness, disgust, guilt,* and ask them to assume the positions appropriate to the word on their card.

- Ask the group, "What attitude does each people represent?

- Ask for each emotion to be named. **5 MIN.**

## INSTRUCTOR NOTES:
- Dale Carnegie in *How to Win Friends and Influence People,* tells a story about a miserable man who moved to Florida. His father gave him a sealed letter and told him not to open it for six months. The unhappy man was miserable in Florida also. In six months he opened his father's letter, which told him that he had taken himself with him when he went to Florida.

**POINT: It's not where you are that makes you happy or unhappy; it's your attitude that determines happiness.** **4 MIN.**

**DEFINITION:**
- Ask participants for **definitions of *Attitude,*** then write on board **"Attitude is how we see things; how we feel about things."** **3 MIN.**

- Attitude is like the steering mechanism in our brains.

## INSTRUCTOR NOTES:

- In life, **IT IS NOT WHAT HAPPENS TO US, BUT HOW WE REACT TO IT THAT COUNTS.** Give example of someone coming in the room and without reason kicking three people in the front row. Would they all react the same way? Why not? They have each been equally offended. **1 MIN.**

- **Point: Each person chooses his/her reactions. There is a pause between stimulus (kick) and response (crying, retaliating, etc.). You can do anything if you change your attitude about life.** **2 MIN.**

## WHY IS ATTITUDE IMPORTANT?

Ask for examples of times when participants were treated poorly in a store by a sales clerk or on the phone by a service representative. Everyone has a story. For teens and young adults it could be they were treated like suspects about to steal from the shelves. How did they feel when treated poorly?

**POINT: Attitude by an employee can adversely affect business.**

**STATISTICS:** (WRITE ON BOARD: 1, 3, 5, 7, 9, 14, 61)
**A Board of Trade Study:** The reason why people change their place of business is:

1% - die
3% - move away
5 & 7% - have relationship with someone who works there
9% - prices too high
14% - shoddy merchandise
**61%** - because of the **attitude** of someone who works there.
**2 MIN.**

**EXAMPLE:** • **FACT:** Success is determined 15% by your skills and 85% by your attitude. It's your attitude, not your aptitude, that determines your altitude. **1 MIN.**

**TESTIMONY:** • Experts say, "A positive attitude is the one characteristic that all successful people have in common."

**1 MIN.**

**POINT: You can control your attitude!**

**INSTRUCTOR NOTES: To prove your point, relate one or more of the following examples of EVIDENCE:**

# 1. • PENDULUM WITH STRING

Take a piece of string about 10 inches long and put both ends together. Put a key or button or piece of jewelry onto the string and let it hang down. Take the two ends of the string between your thumb and first finger, rest your elbow on the table and let the string with its weight dangle.

Tell the class you are going to "think" it to move. Look at the object on the string and move your eyes from left to right and back again. Picture the object moving, and it will move. By thinking and picturing the way you want it to go, the object will move. You can even make it go in circles. There may be minute movements of your fingers, but you are **NOT consciously** moving them.

**POINT: Your thoughts, or attitude, have an effect on your body without your being aware of it.** Have participants try it.

(Approximately 3/4 of the class will have success with this example. People with military or scientific backgrounds may be too analytical to make the pendant move.)
**15 MIN.**

# 2. • FINGERS OR ARMS

Ask participants to clasp hands together, fingers laced on top of one another. Extend your two forefingers toward the ceiling and keep them apart by a distance of 1-2 inches. Tell participants to study their forefingers and imagine there is a tight rubber band around them. Now state in a deliberate tone and in a slow speed, "You can feel that rubber band bringing your fingers closer.and closer.and closer." The smiles and laughter of at least half of your audience will tell you they are getting the message, and their fingers are closing together. About half to two-thirds will respond accordingly.

- Ask participants what prompted fingers to move?

- **POINT: Your thoughts affect your body.**                    **5 MIN.**

# 3. • ARMS

Ask participants to stand, turn, and find a partner. Tell them you are going to demonstrate how our physical actions frequently reflect our mental state, or attitude. Decide which person will be partner "A" and which will be "B". Partner "A" should think about a very positive experience--something that really made them happy and excited. Ask them to close their eyes and nod to their partner when they have a mental picture of that event.

Ask Partner "A's" to raise their right arm out to their side, parallel with the floor, still with their eyes closed. Ask "B's" to move closer to "A's" and place their left hand on "A's" arm. Ask "A's" to state their name aloud and ask "B's" to try and gently push "A's" arm downward as "A" resists. (Partner "A" will be able to withstand the pressure.)

Now ask "B's" to think of a recent experience that was not pleasant at all. Ask "B's" to close their eyes and nod when they have that negative thought in mind. Ask them to raise their right arm as "A's" place their left hand on "B's" arm. Tell "B's" to select a fictitious name and say that aloud, i.e., "My name is John Doe" and tell "A's" to push down while "B's" resist. (In most cases, the arm will easily be pushed downward.)

- Ask what is the impact on your body of being happy and truthful?

- What is the typical impact on your body of feeling negative? Being untruthful?
  **5 MIN.**

## • CAN YOU CONTROL YOUR ATTITUDE?

- Have participants respond? Many will say they cannot.

## • EXAMPLE OF CONTROLLING ATTITUDE:

One night I had a PTO meeting scheduled at my house. The night before the meeting I cleaned my house, plumped my pillows, cleaned the counters--everything was perfect. Because I had to work late the night of the meeting, I came running in 15 minutes before people began arriving. When I walked in and saw my two teenagers, I also saw pretzel pieces on the floor, soda cans on the counters, and flat pillows. I went crazy. "How can you be so inconsiderate? How could you do this to me when you know I have a meeting here tonight."

As I was ranting, the telephone rang, and I picked it up and very nicely said, "Hello."

After I hung up, my daughter looked at me and asked, "How could you?"

"How could I what?"

"How could you change so fast from being angry to being polite?"

That's when I realized I do have control over my attitude. If I were to come knocking at your door tonight, while you were in the midst of an argument with a family member, would you also take my head off? No, you probably would be polite until I left. You would control your attitude.

- **Ask participants if they can relate.** You may receive strong disagreement on this point. They may say it is impossible to control their attitudes, and if they

*Gail A. Cassidy*

are mad, they are mad! If so, ask them if their principal or their boss came to their house personally to deliver an extraordinary reward to them, would they stay angry while their principal or boss was there? Most participants will agree they could control their attitudes under certain circumstances.

**POINT: IF YOU CAN CONTROL YOUR ATTITUDE UNDER ONE CIRCUMSTANCE, YOU CAN CONTROL YOUR ATTITUDE UNDER ALL CIRCUMSTANCES 4 MIN.**

## INSTRUCTOR NOTES: RESEARCH ON ATTITUDE AND FACIAL EXPRESSIONS:

- *The information on the next few pages is primarily adapted from* **Mentally Tough**, Dr. James Loehr and Peter McLaughlin.

For as long as sport has been enjoyed, coaches have told their athletes to develop a "good attitude." As the coaches' saying goes, "Attitudes are the stuff of which champions are made." When teams have negative attitudes, they don't play well and they don't win. With the enthusiasm that accompanies a positive attitude, everything else becomes possible.

Neither in sport nor in business have the researchers found a top performer who is a negative thinker or carries a negative attitude. Top performance and negative attitudes simply do not go together.

Lou Holtz: Notre Dame coach, said, "**Winning is an attitude. Ability is what you're capable of doing. Motivation determines what you do. Attitude determines how well you do it.**"

Everyone knows that mood-altering drugs such as morphine, cocaine, amphetamines, etc., can affect how people feel and act. What many people do not know is that something as simple as frowning can cause negative feelings. In fact, in a series of experiments at the School of Medicine at the University of California at San Francisco in 1983, research subjects were wired to machines similar to polygraphs and were videotaped as their pulse, skin temperature, skin electrical resistance, and muscle tension were measured second-by-second.

In one phase of the study, subjects were told to arrange their facial muscles in certain ways--the frightened-face instructions. In another phase, the subjects were asked to relive emotional experiences.

A facial expression associated with happiness--smiling--produced the same physical changes as did reliving a pleasant emotional experience.

A fearful look, held for ten seconds, caused the same tenseness in the muscles and drop in skin temperature as an actual fearful experience. This also held for professional actors. No matter how practiced you are at controlling your facial expression, the expression will be reflected physically in the same way that an emotional feeling affects the body and its ability to perform.

Further, choosing to adopt a facial expression changes your emotional state very quickly. It can take 30 seconds of reliving a frightening experience to produce the same changes that occurred with ten seconds of grimacing.

**POINT:** Put on a confident smile and you will feel secure and confident. Look angry for a few seconds, and you'll feel angry. Frown, and your entire nervous system will frown with you. **Your emotional state reflects your face every bit as much as your face reflects your emotional state.**

Facial expression, more than any other physical attribute, is a reflection of one's emotional state. Such conscious efforts take a lot of effort for most people--which explains why a skilled poker player pays more attention to the faces at the table than the faces on the cards, or why the best actors and actresses can command astronomical sums for their work.

As nearly as researchers can tell now, the human brain automatically expresses emotions by signaling the facial muscles--it's something built in, and it is apparent very early in life. Babies smile when they're happy, and that occurs months before they have the fine muscle control necessary for similar learned behavior, like speech.

**10 MIN.**

**INSTRUCTOR NOTES: REVERSING THE FLOW:** You smile when you're happy, grimace when you're angry, and frown when you're upset. But it turns out that the transmission of nerve signals runs both ways. That is, you can feel better as a result of smiling, become angry merely by grimacing, and be annoyed just by frowning.

> **SMILING:** "When you are smiling, you are measurably lowering your stress level, boosting your immune system, improving your complexion and lengthening your life, scientists say. No wonder the whole world smiles with you." (-Valerie Monroe, *O Magazine)*

> In the same article, Ms. Monroe states that "on a social level, an honest smile defuses hostility and draws people near you." A recent study at the University of California at Berkeley, published in the Journal of Personality and Social Psychology, found that women who had smiled the most in their college yearbook

photos had happier lives, happier marriages, and fewer personal setbacks in the following 30 years.

"It is even okay to fake a smile. Put on a happy face, and your body, either not knowing the difference or hoping for the best, responds as if the expression were genuine. The act of smiling engages at least three major muscle groups, increasing blood flow to the face and thus helping to create a rosy glow. Laugh heartily and you tone your facial muscles; get downright delirious and you get a serious aerobic workout. Laughter has a protective effect on the immune system by increasing antibody-producing cells and activating virus-fighting T cells."

**EXERCISE:**
- Hold your face as it you were deeply frightened. Raise your eyebrows and pull them together. Now raise your upper eyelids. Stretch your lips horizontally, back toward your ears.

- Hold this position for a minute or so, and you won't be the same person you were two minutes ago. No longer will you be relaxed, comfortable, and adjusted to your environment. Your face will go pale and your skin will cool as blood moves from the surface to the large skeletal muscles, which grow more tense by the moment. Your pupils will dilate and your eyes will become more sensitive to motion. Your heart will beat faster and your blood pressure will rise. In the deeper regions of your central nervous system, the chemical balance changes as epinephrin (adrenaline) enters your bloodstream and begins to transmit impulses among your brain's emotional control centers.

## INSTRUCTOR NOTES:

- By any measure known to science, you are in a state of fear if you hold this facial expression. Something as insignificant as the way you arrange your facial muscles changed your emotional state and thus your body chemistry. Consequently, every other part of you, from the dilated pupils to the changed breathing to the taut muscles within your feet, was also affected.

- It is generally thought that you smile because you feel good. That's true, but so is the reverse. Recent scientific research has proven that you can feel good because you smile.

- When you're smiling, you're measurably lowering your stress level, boosting your immune system, improving your complexion, and lengthening your life, scientists say. No wonder the whole world smiles with you.

**10 MIN.**

## LAUGHTER:

- Laughter is one of best medicines in world. It helps you feel better and is a great preventive medicine. Laughter causes your body to secrete natural hormones into your system. Endorphins are 200 times as powerful as morphine. Laughter gives you a positive orientation. When people laugh, they cannot worry. When you laugh you begin to program yourself toward a more productive level.

- Adults average 12 laughs a day; children laugh over 400 times a day.

**EXERCISE:**
- Think of a very sad or upsetting thing that has happened in your life.
- Smile as warmly as you can.
- Notice your feelings about the event while you're smiling.

**POINT:** No matter what the thought, you cannot fully have the feeling if the physiology doesn't match or if it contradicts the thought. **3 MIN.**

**EXERCISE:**
- Have everyone laugh for 15 seconds. It is almost like doing a 50 yard dash. You feel good physically, emotionally and mentally. **5 MIN.**

**EXAMPLE:**
- NORMAN COUSINS, *Anatomy of an Illness*. When diagnosed with a terminal illness, the author checked into a hotel with Abbott and Costello and other funny videos. He attributes his recovery to laughter.

**POINT: Assume a virtue, if you have it not" and it will be so.** -William Shakespeare
**10 MIN.**

**PRACTICE:** Have the class stand and assume difference body positions (as done previously to indicate attitude).

1. Confident
2. Insecure

3. Elated

4. Depressed

- Notice how you feel when you assume each position.
- Does each position allow you to experience different emotions?
- When you assume a new attitude, the new attitude brings on new perceptions, new feelings, new muscular patterns.
- How did you feel?
- What does this mean to you?
- How can you use it? **10 MIN.**

**POINT:**
- You can change your attitude through body use. Nerve impulses flow both ways.

## VALIDATION:

When you change your **THINKING**, you change your **BELIEFS**;
When you change your **BELIEFS**, you change your **EXPECTATIONS**;
When you change your **EXPECTATIONS,** you change your **ATTITUDE**;
When you change your **ATTITUDE**, you change your **BEHAVIOR**;
When you change your **BEHAVIOR**, you change your **PERFORMANCE**;
When you change your **PERFORMANCE**, you change your **YOUR LIFE!**

from Dr. Walter Doyle Staples, Think Like a Winner, (Pelican Publishing, Gretna, 1991.) **5 MIN.**

# THOUGHTS:

- "Great men," Emerson wrote, "are those who see that thoughts rule the world."

- Thought is the original source of all success, prosperity, and happiness in the world.

- All that you accomplish or fail to accomplish in life is a direct result of the images you hold in your mind.

- You actually think in images and not in words. An image has a much greater impact on your brain than words, reflecting the fact that the nerves from the eye to the brain are twenty-five times larger than the nerves from the ear to the brain.

- Every thought you have has an idea or verbal component, an image or conceptual component and an emotional or feeling component.

- You record information in your mind about all of your experiences in a three-dimensional format: verbal, conceptual, and emotional. This information is collected through your five senses to form the basis for your personal belief system or your understanding of the world in aggregate form as you know it.

- People have in their lives today exactly what they keep telling their mind they want.

- Your physical world today basically reflects all of the thinking you have or have not engaged in up to now.

**LOGIC:** Do you believe the following? (FROM Wayne Dyer's *Erroneous Zones.*)
- **I control my thoughts** (If you don't, who does?)
- **My feelings come from my thoughts** (You can't be upset about something until you hear about it. For example, you can't be excited about winning the lottery until you learn that you have.)
- **Therefore, I control my feelings.** (This concept is a tough one to internalize. How can you distract yourself from negative feelings? You could read, take a walk, talk to friend, go to the mall, get busy, or do anything you enjoy doing. Most of the time you can change your feelings by changing your thoughts.) **10 MIN.**

**POINTS:**
- When you change your thinking, you change your life.

- Your world is basically what your thoughts make of it.
- "Attitudes are more important than facts," according to Dr. Karl Menninger.
- Positive thinking is practical living. It is the most productive and most fulfilling.
- Your reality is what you make it to be. You can train yourself to think more positively by training yourself to choose what you pay attention to and what you say about it, both to yourself and others. **5 MIN.**

**QUOTES: [Post quotations around room to refer to throughout course.]**

- Shakespeare: "We know what we are but know not what we may be."

- Norman Vincent Peale: "Change your thoughts and you change your world."

- Eleanor Roosevelt: "No one can make you feel inferior without your permission."

- Gandhi: "No one can take away your self respect unless you give it to them."

- Shakespeare: "Nothing is either good or bad but thinking makes it so."

- William James: "The greatest discovery of my generation is that human beings can alter their lives by altering their attitudes."

- Henry Ford: "If you think you can or think you cannot, you are right."

- John Lilly: "In the province of the mind, what one believes to be true, either is true or becomes true."

- Chapman: "You keep your positive attitude when you give it away."

**REMEMBER:** • There is a pause between Stimulus and Response.

**POEM:**                    "THOUGHTS ARE THINGS"

I hold it true that thoughts are things;
They're endowed with bodies and breath and wings:
And that we send them forth to fill
The world with good results, or ill.
That which we call our secret thought
Speeds forth to earth's remotest spot,
Leaving its blessings or its woes
Like tracks behind it as it goes.

We build our future, thought by thought,
For good or ill, yet know it not.
Yet so the universe was wrought.
Thoughts is another name for fate;
Choose then they destiny and wait,
For love brings love and hate brings hate.

-Henry Van Dyke                    **3 MIN**.

from Dr. Walter Doyle Staples, *Think Like a Winner,* (Pelican Publishing, Gretna, 1991.)

## HOW CAN YOU CHANGE ATTITUDE? This is the way to do it:

- Shoulders back
- Head up
- Smile
- Positive thoughts/Affirmations                    **2 MIN.**

**INSTRUCTOR NOTES:**

**EXAMPLE:**

- James Mapes, author of Quantum Leap Thinking: When touring colleges as a hypnotist, James would have the participants identify a shy person in the audience, whom he would then invite up to the stage. James would quietly say a few words to this person, who then would display visible confidence. The audience thought it was hypnosis, but all he had told the subject was to stand erect, chin up, shoulders back, walk out to the edge of the stage, and slowly look to the right and to the left."

**3 MIN.**

**INSTRUCTOR NOTES:**

**POINT:**
- Inside your head is where it all starts. It is possible to decide which focus we will use. Just like using a camera, we can focus our mind on what appeals to us. We can see situations as problems or opportunities. A class can be viewed as interesting or a waste of time. Quite simply, we take the pictures of life that we want to take. Nobody owns our attitude. It is exclusively ours. We alone control it--**WHAT POWER!**

**2 MIN.**

# CONCLUDE ATTITUDE:

[Read this essay by Charles Swindoll to participants.]

"The longer I live, the more I realize the impact of attitude on life. Attitude, to me, is more important than facts. It is more important than the past, than education, than money, than circumstances, than failures, than successes, than what other people think or say or do. It is more important than appearance, giftedness or skill. It will make or break a company, a church, a home.

"The remarkable thing is we have a choice every day regarding the attitude we will embrace for that day. We cannot change our past. We cannot change the fact that people will act in a certain way. We cannot change the inevitable. The only thing we can do is play on the one string we have, and that is our attitude.

«I am convinced that life is 10 percent what happens to me and 90 percent how I react to it. And so it is with you. We are in charge of our attitudes."

**4 MIN.**

**Assignment:**
- Remember to practice your talk
- 5x8 cards must be in by the next class as the latest!
- Work on your Planning Sheets

# TESTIMONIALS RELATING TO INCREASED CONFIDENCE

## <u>CONFIDENCE</u>

- First speech: "I was sweating and shaking. I was nervous to get in front of the class. I then felt better when my classmates clapped for me when I was going up. I felt a little better but I was still nervous. When I finished my talk my classmates clapped for me and said I did a good job. I also felt better because they were quiet and they listened to my talk."

- "I gained more confidence when talking in front of an audience."

- "Then I present a show of my own, hear positive comments from my classmates, and feel good about myself. I still don't want to be a center of attention but now I'm more comfortable doing what I have to do."

- "Public Speaking is the best class I have ever taken. I saw the change in people like C and S who were never outspoken and the change in them is incredible. I learned more about my image."

- "I feel I have gotten a lot out of this course. I am confident when speaking in front of a group of people (especially my peers). I know I can get through an interview successfully. In saying all this, it comes as an obvious statement when I say I thoroughly enjoyed this course."

- "As a result of this course, I have gained a confidence before my audience that I have never felt before."

- "I have learned a lot from it because my confidence has grown and now I can't wait to give my next speech."

- "This class has made a big difference in my life. Before Effective Speaking I was a lot shyer than I am now, a couple of months later. The first time I went to make a talk, I was scared to death. I was worried about what the rest of the class would think. Now I feel so comfortable talking in front of people. I actually have a lot more fun giving the talks now that I have overcome my fear."

- "Every one of my talks were successful and each time I felt more confident than the last. Every time I get up to talk now, I feel like I belong up in front. Learning to speak in front of the room increases your confidence, self-esteem and comfort level as well as speaking ability and level of preparation. Effective Speaking is one of the most worthwhile classes I have ever had the pleasure of being in."

- "The way of complimenting and giving positive remarks rather than criticizing has helped make it [speaking] more comfortable and [I am] more willing to do a better speech the next time."

- "Now after taking this course, I can comfortably give a speech without the fear that I used to have. I can now arrange mental notes so I remember what I would like to say. Effective Speaking greatly helped me and I enjoyed taking it this year."

- "This class is important because before I took this class I used to shake and stutter when I got in front of the class. Now people compliment my speaking skills."

*Gail A. Cassidy*

# WEEK TWO

## FAVORITE FUNNY STORY TALK

## <u>TIPS FOR THE WEEK:</u>

4   •   Recognize the specialness of diversity.
5   •   Provide an atmosphere conducive to learning: posters, adages, lighting, safety,.etc.
6   •   Vary your activities. Do something different that they will remember.

ØØØØØØØØØØ

**OBJECTIVES:**     •   To overcome fear

•   To build confidence

•   To learn how to organize talks

•   To learn effective openings

•   To understand use of evidence

•   To learn effective closings

•   To learn how to psyche themselves before a talk

•   To understand more about Attitude

•   To learn how to control Attitude

•   To understand breathing techniques

•   To learn difference between perception and reality

•   To become aware of non-verbal communication

- To understand that what we see may not be what is

- To become more aware of body language cues

**REVIEW:**
- What do you remember about *Attitude*?

- How can you personally relate to what was covered?

- Have you brought your awareness to people and events outside of class? If so, how?

- **Review ISOMETRICS**, No. 1 under "About to Give Talk" on Nervousness Tool Kit sheet. Have participants practice.

**CARDS:**
- Assign each participant a number for their 5 x 8 cards or pages. (It is easier for participants to find a number each time a speaker's name and number are called.)

- Participants: Write assigned number on top, right corner of card/page. Arrange by number.

- Exchange cards with every person in class and give one to instructor.

- **Must have cards or pages with you every session.**

**CRITIQUE:**
- Have enlarged Critique Sheet posted in view of participants.

- Discuss what to look for in each speaker.

- Stress "positives" only and explain why. [If you point out a negative, the speaker will concentrate on that and tend to repeat it.]

- Explain that they will receive at least one recommendation for improvement on their "Planning Sheets."

*Gail A. Cassidy*

- A student's final grade will be determined by how well their written recommendations have been addressed.

**PROCEDURE:**

- As each speaker is called to the front of the room by name and number, he will first give the Planning Sheet to the instructor.

- **Participants clap as soon as speaker's name is called.**

- No podium is to be used for beginning talks.

- For the first talks, notes are not necessary. If a participant's mind goes blank, the instructor can help by referring to the speaker's Planning Sheet and asking appropriate questions. Never allow a student to become flustered or upset because of temporary memory loss.

- The instructor also has one card for each participant on which he/she writes comments as the person talks. Those notes are later transferred to the Planning Sheets and returned to the speaker the next day. **Write two positives and one recommendation for improvement.**

- If you are using grades, a grade must be assigned immediately on the participant's card, or else you will not remember after listening to numerous talks.

- At one minute 50 seconds, use a cricket or say aloud "ten seconds" to indicate they must wind down talk.

- At two minutes, ring bell. If the speaker is in the middle of a sentence, she may end that sentence only.

- **Participants clap as speaker returns to seat.**

- After speaker returns to his seat, he will complete the Self Evaluation sheet and give to the instructor.

**WARMUP:**

Use one of the five exercises in the "Nervousness Tool Kit" before talks each day. **4 MIN.**

**RAP TIME:** Have participants stand and face the person closest to her. Decide which is "a" and which is "b" (the method of selecting could be the tallest, shortest, one with most white or blue or red on their clothes--something fun). This time the "a's" get to go first. What they are doing is practicing their talks to see if they have too much time or too little time. Time them carefully, then change speakers. Have second person practice his talk. This is done at the beginning of each new round of talks

**TALKS:**
- Ask for a volunteer to give the first talk. Explain that the first person to volunteer is the one who will benefit the most because he or she will be able to relax for the rest of the week.

- All participants: When instructor calls the name and number of next speaker, take the appropriate card out of your pile by number as person walks to the front of the room.

- **CLAP.**

- Look at Critique sheet on wall or in your packet to remind yourself what to look for as the speaker delivers his/her talk.

- Look for what the speaker is doing right and write it on his card.

- Ten second warning.

- Bell at two minutes.

- **CLAP** as speaker returns to her seat.

- After each talk, ask participants for what they liked.

- Take about three responses.

- Instructor gives **one** pointed positive. (*Sincerity* is most important here in order to maintain credibility. If you cannot think of a positive comment, you can always comment on her "courage to give the talk" or how "he earned the right to give this talk." A false compliment will adversely affect your credibility with future speakers.)

- Participants and instructor write their own individual positive comment(s) on speaker's card.

## FEEDBACK THROUGHOUT CLASS:

- What have you noticed about previous speakers?

- How does that make you feel?

- To those who have given their presentations, "How did you feel while speaking?

- "How did you feel about being critiqued after speaking?"

**NEW MATERIAL:** • **From Participant Packets: [The following four pages in the Student Manual should be covered every class period until the class is totally familiar with the information.]**

1. • **Organization of Talks**: Self explanatory. Review thoroughly with participants.

2. • **Openings**: Encourage participants to try a variety of openings. Stress the purpose of openings. [Practice with a partner.]

3. • **Evidence**: The beginning talks will use mostly experiences or stories. With more experience, participants should be urged to use a variety of types of evidence, especially in the talks to persuade, to sell, and the final exam. [Give example.]

4. • **Closings:** Remind participants that their close should trigger audience applause.

• For the first talk, have students write and practice a variety of openings and closings for their next talk. Have them practice with a partner.

**ASSIGNMENT:**     • **NEGOTIATING/ROLE PLAYING TALKS NEXT WEEK** [Use Negotiating Planning sheet] Explain that each speaker is to take a role playing sheet before they leave class and be ready to defend position next session. Request that participants **not** share their role with anyone.

NAME:_____ DATE: _____

# PLANNING SHEET FOR
# NEGOTIATING/ROLE PLAYING
*[PACKET]*

**WHAT IS YOUR POSITION?**

_____

**WHAT IS THE VALUE OF THIS TO THIS AUDIENCE?:**

_____

**OPENING: (Use exact wording)** _____

_____

_____

**EVIDENCE TO VALIDATE YOUR POSITION:**

**#1:** _____

**#2:** _____

**#3:** _____

**#4:** _____

**#5:** _____

**CLOSE: (Use exact wording)** _____

**POINT:** _____

**BENEFIT TO LISTENERS IN KNOWING HOW TO DO THIS:**

_____

# CASE STUDY:
# PROBLEMS AT THE "Y"

## from perspective of
## ALICE, THE DAYCARE WORKER

Alice is a daycare worker with a "Y" located about 45 minutes from her home. A well-qualified person, she is newly employed and knows she has to make a good impression.

Unfortunately, this morning before work, Alice woke up late because the electricity went out during the night. On top of that, the shower ran only ice-cold water. On the way to work, Alice was trying to make up for lost time and was stopped by the police and given a very high fine ticket plus points for exceeding the speed limit by 20 miles.

Alice arrives at work late. Her supervisor is unhappy not only because Alice is late, but also because two other daycare workers called in sick and she cannot find replacements, and today is "parent's day" where Mom and Dad come in to see how their little child is doing in nursery school. Alice has to double her workload for the day.

The first person to arrive at the "Y" is Mrs. Van Dyke whom everyone is familiar with. She is a regular and is a complainer about everything associated with the "Y" even though she comes daily. Alice politely takes care of her but loses time listening to Mrs. Van Dyke's complaints.

By eleven o'clock Alice has seen numerous parents, is exhausted and the parents are lining up complaining because they've been waiting so long. When Joe Smith arrives at the counter and starts being verbally abusive, Alice explodes and tells him a thing or two. Alice's supervisor overhears the tirade and asks Alice to come in the back.

**What should Alice do?**

# PROBLEMS AT THE "Y"

## from perspective of
## JOE, THE PARENT

Joe Smith is the father of five young children. His wife died recently from cancer, and he is devastated. He is an iron worker who cannot depend on continuous employment and lives in constant fear of not being able to care for his children.

This morning Joe was at work when a coworker dropped a heavy piece of metal on Joe's knee as he was bending to weld an iron joist. Joe's pain is surpassed only by his fear of being laid up and unable to earn money and his fear of disappointing his kids in daycare.

He arrived at the "Y" at 8:30 a.m. for his parent/teacher interview. It is now after 11:00 a.m., and still no one has even called his name. This cool-looking, pretty daycare worker is taking her sweet time making idle chitchat with other parents as he sits there in pain, losing precious time off the job.

Enough is enough. At 11:05 after watching the idle chitchat continue, Joe hobbles up to the desk and lets them know what he thinks in no uncertain terms. That sassy broad has nerve to answer him back in that tone of voice!

**What should Joe do?**

# PROBLEMS AT THE "Y"

## from perspective of
## <u>MRS. JONES, THE SUPERVISOR</u>

Today started like any other. Mrs. Jones got the kids off to school and got to work in plenty of time. Unfortunately, there were two messages for her. Two of the scheduled daycare workers called in sick. Mrs. Jones phoned her list of substitutes but could find no one at home. Worse things could happen, she thought.

Mrs. Jones had great confidence in the new girl, Alice, and the rest of the staff. It would be tough, but they would get through the day.

The "Y" opens and the new girl, Alice, is not yet there. Normally, Mrs. Jones would not be that upset, but this early in the day is a very bad time to have parents backing up, especially on this special teacher/parent day. Alice arrived in a harried state, apologized and started to work immediately.

At 11:05, Mrs. Jones hears loud, abusive language from a very angry man, followed by equally loud, abusive language from her new hiree, Alice.

**What should Mrs. Jones do?**

*Gail A. Cassidy*

# EVALUATION

Looking at "**Be the Best That You Can Be**" tips booklet, find tips that would be applicable to this situation.

Review reasons why Joe is right.

Review reasons why supervisor is right.

Review reasons why Alice is right.

How should this situation be handled? All of the scenes have occurred, now how can Joe be placated? Alice? Mrs. Jones? Is it possible?

Act out the next scene, with the goal of placating all three people.

# ORGANIZATION OF TALKS
### [PACKET]

Dottie Walters, a renowned speaker and trainer of speakers, recommends what she calls the "five finger" talk. **The opening is the pinky, three points, and end with a strong thumb.**

Keeping that image in mind, be mindful of what every talk must have to be effective.

1. **OPENING: See examples on Openings Page.** You need to capture your audience's attention immediately with a catchy opening.

2. **UP TO THREE POINTS: Use evidence (See Evidence Sheet) to prove your point.** Use a story, statistics, quotes--whatever is necessary to bring your point home to the audience.

3. **CLOSE: includes three parts:**

   1 • **State ACTION audience should take.** Why else would you be talking to them? You want them to take action, even if your intent is to entertain, their action is laughter.
   2 • **Restate your point and action needed.**
   3 • **State benefit to those listening to your talk.** The following is an example:

# TALK

**TITLE:** "Road rage has potentially grave consequences"

***OPENING WITH EVIDENCE:*** About a month ago, I was driving to work, when all of a sudden, a van passed me on the right side, got in front of me, and slammed on the brakes. I almost slammed into him. I was so angry I wanted to swear at him or better yet, tap his fender and see how he liked it. We came to a dead stop. People got out of their cars--the perfect opportunity to tell this man what I thought of his driving skills. Fortunately, I held my tongue because what I could not see was a young boy who had run out into the street to get his ball and had been grazed by the car in front of the van. I also quickly learned that this man had been so impatient because he was trying to get his vastly pregnant wife to the hospital before the baby arrived. I am so glad I did not act on my initial impulse.

**CLOSING:**

1. **RESTATE POINT AND ACTION.** Restate point: *"My point is "See things from another's perspective" or "Patience is a virtue" or "Road rage has potentially grave consequences."*
2. **BENEFIT:** (What the listeners will receive by doing what is asked for in the POINT STEP.)
   *"Because if you do, you may prevent considerable embarrassment."*

(Please note that this talk contained a specific incident out of the class member's life. The speaker asked for action and then gave a benefit for the listeners resulting from this action.)

# Let's Examine the Steps of the Speaking Formula

**OPENING: Capture audience attention.**

**YOUR STORY: (up to three points, using evidence)** *Should be an experience from your own life--one that taught you a lesson.*

**THE POINT** (Answers the question: *What do you want us to do (that you think will help us?)*

**ACTION STEP(S):** *Why should we do it?*

**BENEFIT:** *How will we benefit if we do what you ask? e.g., what's in it for me?*

# OPENINGS
*[PACKET]*

- **TALK OBJECTIVES:**
  - To inform
  - To entertain
  - To persuade
  - To inspire

- **Tell them what you are going to tell them.**

- **Startling statement:** "Look to your right and left. One will not be here by the end of the semester."

- **Quote an authority:** "The fire captain said the most common area for fires is the kitchen."

- **Use a prop.** If selling, show your product. If a prop relates to your talk, use it.

- **Compliment your audience.** Find out something special about the group and relate it to them.

- **Ask a question.** Rhetorical: "Are you afraid of losing your job?" Direct: "How many of you have slept through your alarm?"

- **Ask your audience to do something.** "Stretch. Introduce yourself to the person next to you. Stand."

- **Tell a story or joke** (if you can).

- **Show a graphic on an overhead.**

## PURPOSE:

1. To get an immediate response from your audience.
2. To release tension.
3. To build confidence.
4. To get a perspective on your audience by their responses.
5. **To capture audience attention.**

*Gail A. Cassidy*

# EVIDENCE
### [PACKET]

**CITING AN EXPERT:** Quoting someone in authority.

**FACTS/STATISTICS:** Numbers, comparisons, percentages.

**PROPS:** A visual, picture, object, drawing, etc.

**ACTION:** Act out how something works

**METAPHORS:** Making a direct comparison. Relate to something to which audience can relate, i.e., *the car skidded the length of a football field.*

**STORIES:** A story about something that has happened to you or to someone you know, a case study, or an historical event.

### There are different types of stories you can use:

- **Vignettes:** brief, descriptive incident or scene which can be told in a minute or so. Historical events, examples, case studies.
- **Life and death stories:** stories of great loss, hardship, or pain. Olympic athletes, cancer survivors, people who have overcome incredible odds tell their stories. These stories deal with life and death and can be used to teach a profound lesson.
- **Embarrassing moment story:** Funny stories which allow us to be funny. Use to humanize yourself so audience can identify with you.
- **News stories:** Current events that can be used to prove your point and which add to your credibility.
- **Personal stories:** Ordinary experiences that prove your point. adapted from Doug Stevenson's *Never Be Boring Again!*

## PEOPLE LOVE STORIES!!

# MORE ON STORIES AS EVIDENCE
*[PACKET]*

Using a story as evidence has worked well for a number of famous speakers. Dale Carnegie employed stories when he gave a talk at the YMCA early in his career after he had exhausted his topic and still had time left. He told a story about his topic, and his speech was remembered, and Carnegie went on to build an empire on speaking.

In a *Network Marketing Lifestyles* article, the headline reads "The cornerstone of Gove's teaching is simple--the key to making a good presentation is to make a point and tell a story. [Bill] Gove is masterful at it; his comedic timing is impeccable. Says Gove, 'I never look at myself as a public speaker. . . sounds an awful lot like a government job. I like being known as a storyteller.'"

The article goes on to say that "each story has a life of its own. It might be only three or four minutes long, but each one has a premise, a problem, and a payoff or lesson learned--just like a regular speech. We learn to connect mini-speeches together, rather than face the horrible task of sitting down and organizing one long 40-minute speech.

This approach comes from Mark Twain . . . It's, 'Let me tell you a story,' and then, part way into the story, you say, 'Let me give you an example. . .' - and of course, the example is always the personal story."

Similar to Carnegie, Gove came across his style accidentally. His boss announced that he was going to present a half-hour speech on closing the sale. Gove was terrified. "I thought, 'You must be crazy! A half hour on closings?' I didn't think I could come up with more than ten minutes worth. I was wrong; it was worse. I put together my talk on closing--and it came out to about five minutes. . . so I added 25 minutes of Uncle Phil's stories.' The talk was a sensation. Twenty-five minutes of Maine vignettes a la Uncle Phil wrapped around a central theme ("closing the sale") gave Bill Gove the platform for a lifetime of stories that teach and train as they entertain."

The point is audiences tune out to "thou shalts" but tune in to a good story. Stories can be supplemented with statistics, analogies, etc., but it is the story and the point that they will remember.

# CLOSINGS
### [PACKET]

**CHOOSE YOUR CLOSING ACCORDING TO THE OBJECTIVE OF YOUR TALK.**

- Tell them what you told them--**SUMMARY OF MAIN POINTS.**

- Ask audience to take action.

- Challenge the audience to take a specific action, e.g., contribute to a charity, floss daily, be careful on the slopes, take care of your parents.

- Refer to your opening statement. This ties the talk together.

- Dramatize your point.

- Restate the key benefit of your talk.

- Ask a rhetorical question.

- Use an appropriate quote.

- Make an observation.

- Give a final motivating statement.

- Combine techniques, e.g., tell a story, recite a poem, and quote an authority.

**"Wind up with a line, or anecdote, a proverb, a quotation or some other memorable piece of copy that leaves your audience laughing or thoughtful-- depending on the subject of your address."** *How To Be the Life of the Podium* by Sylvia Simmons.

# CLOSE SHOULD TRIGGER AUDIENCE APPLAUSE

# ENJOY THE ACCOLADES!!

# AFFIRMATIONS

## [PACKET]

To counter nervousness, it is essential to understand that you can *drown out* the discouraging silent voices that often speak in your mind--those voices that make you doubt yourself and make you feel incapable of speaking in front of a group. We get what we focus on emotionally. Focus on a relaxed, dynamic presentation.

**AFFIRMATIONS** are positive, present tense statements which are indicative of your intentions. Make a written list of affirmations you can refer to each time you are about to speak.

To use **AFFIRMATIONS, just speak ALOUD to yourself.** Again, the words must be positive and in the present tense, as if what you are saying is already so, e.g., "I am totally prepared." "The audience loves my talk." "This is the best talk I've ever delivered." "I am a dynamic speaker." "I am confident." Expect success and you will be successful.

Carefully plan each word you want to hear. State the words clearly and concisely. Speak them with authority, as though you are lecturing an audience of hundreds who have come to hear your words of wisdom.

Painting this picture in your mind's eye will give you the feeling of confidence. The words will follow. Act "as if" you already have positive, confident thoughts, and they will follow. In your mind, see the audience responding well to your talk.

Persistence in using **AFFIRMATIONS** and visualizing them in your mind's eye will prove highly rewarding. Assign yourself daily "private time" for this exercise. Each day it will become easier until it will be ingrained as a habit and become "you" without conscious thought.

Norman Vincent Peale said, "You are not what you think you are, but what you think, you are." Think about that!

*Gail A. Cassidy*

- **New topic to be used in an early session as time allows.**

# LESSON: PERCEPTION IS REALITY

## 55% OF MESSAGE COMES FROM THE BODY

### EXERCISE:

- **PURPOSE:** To demonstrate that verbal communication may become awkward for us when nonverbal gestures or actions are prohibited.

**PROCEDURE:**

- Have a student turn to someone seated nearby and talk about anything that comes into his head for two minutes--something that interests him, a TV show, a movie, what he did since getting up this morning--anything to keep talking for two minutes. He will be notified when the first two minutes are up.

- **Switch speakers.** The listener now has an opportunity to speak for two minutes on anything that interests her.

- **Stop:** Have each student take up to one minute to tell what they noticed about the other's nonverbal behavior: for example, the person kept fiddling with a pencil or tapping fingers, etc.

- After each person has received a "critique" from her partner, continue the conversation, each taking two minutes, but now they must make a conscious effort to use no nonverbal movements.

**QUESTIONS:**

1. Were most of you really aware of your nonverbal movements in first conversation?

2. Did you find any of your partner's gestures distracting or even annoying?

3. How did it "feel" when you were forced into strictly verbal conversation? Was the communication as effective without your gestures? **15 MIN.**

**GENERAL RULES FOR GESTURING:**

1. Use gestures when using action words.

2. Less is more. Use gestures to emphasize major points.

**PROBLEMS:** **[Write on board "PROBLEMS" and the following two statements]**

- We Cannot <u>NOT</u> Communicate.

- "We are not always perceived in the manner we intend."

**EXAMPLES:**
- Can you give me an example of how someone misunderstood you?

- "What perception do you have of a person with tattoos, black leather jackets, high heels and jeans?

- Are you always right?

**CAUSES:** The reason people are not always perceived as they want to be is because of NON-VERBAL COMMUNICATION.

- **UNIVERSAL PROBLEM:** There are two misguided assumptions about communicating:

(1) What you see is what everyone else sees and

(2) You have direct access to reality.

**Emphasize: YOU CANNOT <u>NOT</u> COMMUNICATE.**

- Body language can speak louder than words. Over 90% of how people are perceived is directly related to body language, not what is verbalized.

- **Ralph Waldo Emerson said, "What you are speaks so loudly that I cannot hear what you say."**

**INSTRUCTOR NOTES:** [On board write the numbers 55%, 38% and 7% and explain percentages.]

## NON-VERBAL COMMUNICATION

- <u>**55% of the message comes from the body.**</u> Ask, "Has anyone ever gone home and known immediately, without saying a word, that their parent, sibling, special other was in a bad mood? How did you know that?" Answer: their body language.

- <u>**38% of the message comes from the voice**</u>--intonation, pitch, speed. Example: "Nice sweater" spoken with sarcasm is not a compliment although the words are.

- The right brain is an indicator of emotional response to what is thought.

- <u>**7% of the message comes from the words**</u>. (The left brain deals with words - indicator of what is being thought)

**10 MIN.**

**PRACTICE: EVERYONE FREEZE:** note posture, facial expressions.

- What is being communicated non-verbally? **2 MIN.**

**PRACTICE: ASK FOR VOLUNTEER:** Recite alphabet while attempting to communicate each of the following: anger, happiness, fear, jealousy, love, nervousness, pride, sadness, satisfaction, sympathy - once facing audience; once with back to audience. What did you notice?
**5 MIN.**

**INSTRUCTOR NOTES: EVIDENCE: Nixon-Kennedy debate.**

In the Nixon-Kennedy debate (1960), radio listeners gave the edge to Nixon. However, those who watched the debate on television widely concluded that Nixon lost the debate (and, consequently, an extremely close election) because of his looks (five o'clock shadow, posture), his actions (eyes, nervous perspiration), and the sound of his voice (nervousness), and not because of argumentative substance. The television camera, experts said, was relentless in exposing Nixon's shortcomings.

Kennedy, they said, had more skilled advisors and make-up people to take advantage of the then fledgling political medium.

Nixon's deficiencies in all three areas--looks, action, and voice--made it difficult for TV viewers to concentrate on substance, and remain objective.

## POINT: Sounds, words, delivery--together they create your speech image. 4 MIN.

### VISUALS: (55%) (PICTURES IN APPENDIX)

**(1) PRETTY GIRL/WITCH** - What we call our view of life is a shifting image, not a continuous reality. At different times we choose one pattern to look at rather than another, but neither is more real than the other. Reality is not one picture, but two. We cannot see them together, but they are both there. Since we can never see both images at once, it is important to reserve final judgments and evaluations, remembering that every situation is part witch and part pretty girl. **3 MIN.**

**(2) VASE OR PROFILE? (Could be either)**

**(3) WHICH ARROW IS LONGER? (Both are the same.)**

**(4) WHAT DOES THIS SAY? (FLY)**

**(5) Perceptual misreadings:** On the board draw three large triangles and in each write the following, making sure you get in the extra word in each:

| Barefoot | Snake | Busy |
|----------|-------|------|
| in the | in the | as a |
| the park. | the grass | a beaver. |

First and second graders do better seeing the extra word because they see individual words rather than group words. Faster, more accomplished readers make this mistake more readily than slower, less skillful ones. **5 MIN.**

## INSTRUCTOR NOTES: Learn the following stories to tell class throughout the course to make a nonverbal communication point each time the occasion merits a story.

### (6) DINER/KIDS 2 MIN.

One day I was having breakfast at the diner when a man with his three young girls came in. They sat in a booth adjoining mine, a half wood, half glass partition between us. I was reading my paper, and the little girls kept leaning over the partition, making noise, jumping up and down. They were really annoying.

*Gail A. Cassidy*

The lady sitting next to them on the other side finally got fed up and said, "Sir, your children are going to hurt themselves." He looked at her without expression and then said sadly, "Oh, I'm sorry. We just came from the hospital where I learned that their mother is terminally ill."

WOW! Did we ever see the situation, the annoyance, from a different perspective.

**POINT**: What we see may not be what is.                                             **3 MIN.**

## (7) BEAR IN CAVE

Two men were walking across a field when they felt the ground begin to shake. They turned around and saw a bull bearing down on them. One man ran to the nearest tree and swung himself up and watched as his friend ran down the hill, the bull coming closer and closer. At the bottom of the hill, the friend suddenly disappeared. There was a cave at the bottom of the hill.

The man in the tree watched as his friend came back out and the bull again charged him. He ran back in, then came out. The bull again charged, and he again ran back in. This continued for quite some time until the bull got tired and walked away over the hill.

The friend climbed down from the tree, met up with his friend and asked, "Why didn't you stay in the cave?" "I couldn't," he said. "There was a bear in the cave."

**POINT:** What you see may not be what is. The next time someone doesn't speak to you, just remember, there may have been a bear in his or her cave.

## (7) Clyde Von Olsen's Talking Horse

At the turn of the century there was a man, Clyde Von Olsen, who owned what he claimed was a talking horse. The horse could add numbers and come up with the right answer.

In order to test this claim, a panel of judges convened and put the horse through various tests. The horse correctly answered all of the questions. The panel thought that perhaps the instructor was giving him the answers so Von Olsen was dismissed. The horse still gave the correct answers by pawing the ground the correct number of times. The panel had to conclude that this indeed was a most unusual horse, a talking horse.

Many people, however, were not satisfied with that answer and convened another panel. They again removed Von Olsen from the stable area, but the horse still pawed the ground the correct number of times. Finally, they removed everyone from the room and gave the questions to the horse over a loudspeaker. The horse could not answer. WHY?

The conclusion of the panel was that the horse could sense from the minutely subtle reactions of the people in the room when he got the answer correct and he would stop pawing the ground.

**POINT: People emit subtle non-verbal clues which others pick up on.**

**4 MIN.**


## (8) Read aloud The BLIND MAN & ELEPHANT (See attached)

**4 MIN.**


**POINT:** • **We don't all see the same thing.**
• **What we see may not be what is.**

# THE BLIND MEN AND THE ELEPHANT
## [PACKET]

It was six men of Indostan
To learning much inclined,
Who went to see the Elephant
(Though all of them were blind),
That each by observation
Might satisfy his mind.
The First approached the Elephant,
And happening to fall
Against his broad and sturdy side,
At once began to bawl:

"God bless me! but the Elephant
Is very like a wall!"
The Second, feeling of the tusk,

Cried, "Ho! what have we here
So very round and smooth and sharp?

To me 'tis mighty clear
This wonder of an Elephant
Is very like a spear!"
The Third approached the animal,
And happening to take
The Squirming trunk within his hands,
Thus boldly up he spake:

"I see," quoth he, "the Elephant
Is very like a snake!"
The Fourth reached out an eager hand,
And felt about the knee

"What most this wondrous beast is like
Is mighty plain," quoth he:

"Tis clear enough, the Elephant
Is very like a tree!"
The Fifth who chanced to touch the ear,

Said: "E'en the blindest man
Can tell what this resembles most;
Deny the fact who can,
This marvel of an Elephant
Is very like a fan!"
The Sixth no sooner had begun
About the beast to grope,
Then seizing on the swinging tail
That fell within his scope,

"I see," quoth he, "the Elephant
Is very like a rope!"
And so these men of Indostan
Disputed loud and long,
Each in his own opinion
Exceeding stiff and strong,
Though each was partly in the right,
And all were in the wrong!

-John Godfrey Saxe

*Gail A. Cassidy*

NAME:_____ DATE: _____

# PLANNING SHEET FOR
# MY FAVORITE PERSON
### [PACKET]

**WHAT PERSON ARE YOU GOING TO TALK ABOUT?** _____

_____

**WHAT IS THE VALUE OF THIS TO THIS AUDIENCE?** _____

_____

_____

_____

**OPENING: (Use exact wording)** _____

_____

_____

_____

**STEPS IN MOMENT:**

1. _____

#2: _____

#3: _____

#4: _____

**CLOSE: (Use exact wording)** _____

_____

_____

**POINT:** _____

**BENEFIT TO LISTENERS IN KNOWING HOW TO DO THIS:** _____

_____

_____

_____

### EYE COMMUNICATION: WHAT DO YOU FEEL THE
### FOLLOWING CONVEY? (There are no wrong answers.)

1. **Blinking**: surprise or attention
2. **Winking**: confidentiality or flirtation
3. **Widening eyes:** amazement or appetite
4. **Closed:** from sorrow to simple concentration
5. **Stare:** apathy or boredom, fascination or wonder; incomprehension or disbelief; cold eyes of aggression; bold eyes of sexual attraction
6. **Shift sideways:** deception or doubt
7. **Lowered eyes**: guilt, embarrassment, modesty, obedience

**5 MIN.**

## • <u>Glasses together</u>

If I were to come to a party one of the participants was having and put my glass of soda on the table, touching one of your glasses, what would you do? Most of you would, out of politeness, move your glass away. HOWEVER, were I a gorgeous 16-year old who sat down and did the same thing with my glass, would you move yours? Probably not.

**POINT:** We all have a space, approximately 18 inches, that we like people to stand away from us. In this instance, my glass would have been invading your space.

Some space issues are determined by custom. In the Mid-East, men stand much closer than 18 inches while talking. In our culture, standing that close would make us feel very uncomfortable.

**4 MIN.**

## • <u>Triangle: eyes, nose, mouth</u>

During an interview, the interviewer will normally look at the applicant's eyes, nose, mouth. This is done unconsciously, and the applicant is not even aware of it. However, if the interviewer lowers his eyes and goes eyes, nose, chin, the applicant feels something is not comfortable but is unable to figure out what it is. And, if the interviewer goes eyes, nose, neck, this is the beginning of flirtation.

The actions of interviewers and applicants are recorded secretly in order to obtain this type of information. Cameras can be located behind each in order to record verbal and nonverbal communication.

**POINT:** Another person's non-verbal actions can sometimes be felt by us, even if we can't figure out what happened.

**3 MIN.**

## • <u>Eyebrow flash</u>

If I were to see you in the hall, a natural reaction would be a momentary lifting of my eyebrows as I say, "Hi John." However, if my husband were coming down the hall, I may lift my brows and hold them up as I more seductively say, "Hi Tom."

Think about the times you have seen someone to whom you were attracted. What happens to your brows? They go up. Be aware this week. **2 MIN.**

**BODY LANGUAGE: (Cues only)** reinforces facial communication. Also communicates attitude. **1 MIN.**

**EXAMPLE:** 50,000 baseball fans see a close play and interpret the umpire's call according to the team they are rooting for. **2 MIN.**

**PRACTICE: SHAKING HANDS:** Go around the room and shake every hand and comment on type of shake, or ask each member of the class to shake hands with another person, demonstrating the following:

1. A firm, confident handshake

2. A limp "dead-fish" handshake

3. A very active, pump-handle shake

4. A delicate, fingertip handshake

5. The "bruiser," or bone-crusher. **5 MIN.**

**DISCUSS:**

- Ask their experience with each.

- What other behaviors, nonverbal and verbal, would you expect to go with each kind of handshake?

- Did you adopt a "role" when you attempted each kind of handshake - a role that seemed appropriate for the kind of hand clasping being attempted?

- Are there postures, head positions, facial expressions, and verbal reinforcements for the handshakes?

- Taking each type of handshake, discuss signals which would logically accompany each.

- Where did you learn to do that? **5 MIN.**

**PRACTICE:** Convey warm or cold via body.

- Warm - shift toward the other person, smile, maintain direct eye contact, keep hands still.

- Cold - look away, slump, drum fingers, refrain from smiling.

- **DISCUSS DIFFERENCES**. Of what value is there in knowing this? **5 MIN.**

**PRACTICE:**

- Watch parts of TV programs with the sound turned muted. Notice how skilled certain actors or entertainers are in enhancing their messages with nonverbal activity. Notice specifically if they:

1. Use exaggerated facial expressions.

2. Touch other people in some way.

3. Make special use of hand gestures.

4. Use the space in which they are communicating (moving closer to or away from other people.

5. Seem to move naturally and comfortably, like "real" people.

- You may find that some performers you thought were quite skilled turn out to depend almost entirely on their verbal messages to make a point.

- In which kinds of programs did you find the performers most adept at nonverbal communication - comedy? drama? action programs? news presentations? commercials? **4 MIN.**

**CONSIDER THIS:** • To achieve control and charisma, executives must develop a "physical game plan," according to management consultant Debra Benton. Says she: "Walk slowly and purposefully. Plant some pauses along the way."

- Notice: Posture matters. Slouching paints one picture; ramrod straight paints another, and shoulders back and relaxed paints the best picture.
- Everyone has a choice regarding the image they desire to portray.

**MIRRORING:** • Copying gestures is a fine idea: "When talking to Mr. Big, try to emulate whatever he does. It's instant rapport. Use hand gestures. You will appear more charismatic. When walking downstairs, look not down but straight ahead to project the image of being levelheaded. Of course, this could also be an instruction for falling down." "Body Language: Teaching the Right Strut."                    **4 MIN.**

**PRACTICE:** • **Participant Packet: 26 nonverbal communication gestures and discuss. (SEE ATTACHED)**                    **15 MIN.**

• **Body Language Cues #13:** Females, be aware of tilting your head to the side in business situations. The gesture connotes "cute" and can lessen your credibility and/or be construed as being flirtatious.

• Now that students are familiar with body language, have them pair off and face one another for one minute with no talking, no communicating in any way.

• What happened? Ask what their partners communicated. How did they communicate that? Did they look at you, away from you, smile, giggle, shift from one leg to another? How did you read your partner's reaction?

• **POINT:** You can read a person without words.

# BODY LANGUAGE CUES

*[PACKET]*

*Instructor Answer Copy*

## WHAT <u>COULD</u> THE FOLLOWING GESTURES MEAN?

1. Tapping of fingers--(I)
2. Shrugging of shoulders--(disinterest)
3. Wringing of hands--(I-N)
4. Clenched fist(s)--(D)
5. Open hands, palms up, in front of body--(O)
6. Arms crossed on chest--(D/cold, etc.)
7. Walking fast, chin held high, arms swinging--(C)
8. Shuffling walk, head low-(Sad, depressed)
9. Palm held to cheek--(surprise)
10. Stroking chin--(R)
11. Touching, rubbing nose--(S)
12. Hands on Hips--(defiance or comfort)
13. Head titled to side--(O)
14. Steepling of hands--(C)
15. Peering over glasses--(R)
16. Pacing--(I)
17. Pinching bridge of nose--(tired)
18. Sitting on edge of chair--(I)
19. Crossed kicking leg--(boredom)
20. Pointing of index finger--(F)
21. Poor eye contact--(I)
22. Sideways glance--(S)
23. Unbuttoned coat--(O)
24. Rubbing eyes--(S)
25. Playing with hair--(I)
26. Hand covering mouth--(I)

## NEXT TO EACH NUMBER, WRITE THE FIRST LETTER OF WHAT EACH ACTION REPRESENTS TO YOU, USING THE FOLLOWING AS A GUIDE:

**(D)** - Defensiveness

**(S)** - Suspicious

**(C)** - Confidence

**(F)** - Frustration

**(R)** - Reflective

**(O)** - Openness and Cooperation

**(I)** - Insecurity and Nervousness

## Notice how many different meanings each could have. Body language cues are one part of the message.

*Gail A. Cassidy*

ØØØØØØØØØØ

# TESTIMONIALS RELATED TO SELF ESTEEM
## SELF ESTEEM

- "This class, hands down, has boosted my confidence. I especially like that all the comments were positive and no negativity at all was used. In this class I felt more in charge than others but yet still being the student."

- All of us made blunders but it was worth it. This class does not just work while speaking to a whole bunch of people. It also helps you one on one.
  The second benefit of public speaking was learning how to be yourself to get through to people. Each talk showed a different side of our personality. That is just let me be myself."

- "One thing that is great about this class is that I have an advantage over everyone who has not taken it. After I was finished with my talk, I received so many compliments about how I looked so calm and I kept everyone's attention. It felt good to know that I did keep their attention without making a fool of myself and also the fact that I now know that I can handle talking or teaching kids my age and older."

- Leaving this class I feel my self-esteem and confidence has really gone up big time."

- "The best part about Effective Speaking is pointing out the positives in a person's talk. [The instructor] lets you know all talents you have and makes you feel more confident about these talents."

- "[The instructor] always gave comments that boosted our self-esteem and gave us the will to do well."

- "After the class I felt more comfortable about myself. It really picks up your self-esteem."

- "It [Effective Speaking] made us see that it is possible to pick out something positive in everyone. It also helped us to point out the pluses in ourselves before putting ourselves down."

- "The most important aspect of the speech class is that it builds up your self-esteem and it will make you a stronger person. That was the case for me. My fear of speaking in front of large groups of people declined rapidly."

- "Because of positive feedback, participants don't fear criticisms. Everyone builds each other's self-esteem by keeping an optimistic atmosphere and giving support. This is very important in reaching our full potential."

- "I got a lot out of Effective Speaking. When I first started the course, I was shy and didn't open up to people I didn't trust. I also had stage fright. I was always worried about what people were thinking about me, whether it be my voice, which was always made fun of in grammar school, or my clothes, which I always tried to make perfect. I learned to change all those things that I hated and enjoyed meeting and learning about new people while in this course.

  My first speech was rather terrible. I mumbled and didn't speak very loud. I moved my feet and played with my arms and sleeves. I was glad for the positive feedback I got because it made me realize that I didn't do as bad as I thought and I needed to do work on a few things and I changed those habits."

# WEEK THREE

## NEGOTIATING/ROLE PLAYING TALK

## TIPS FOR THE WEEK

7 • Remember, humans of any age cannot listen and absorb for extended periods of time. 20-25 minutes maximum/break/continue.

8 • Get participants involved with teaching. Everyone has something special to offer.

9 • Becoming the teacher is when you learn. -Covey

ØØØØØØØØØØ

**OBJECTIVES:**

• To reinforce the messages of non-verbal communication, specifically, 38% of the message comes from the voice.

• To become comfortable with relaxation exercises from Nervousness sheet.

• To have participants understand another person's point of view.

• To learn importance of word use through examples given by the instructor.

• To understand vocal cues.

• To understand the importance of congruence.

• To learn importance of organizing ideas.

**REVIEW:**

• Participants: How aware were you of people's body
• language after last week's class.

• Were you aware of your own?                    **5 MIN.**

| **WARM-UP:** | • Choose one exercise from "Nervousness" sheet and have participants do. |

| **RAP TIME:** | • Pair off and one side practice talk, then switch. |

| **AFFIRMATIONS:** | • Give yourself a silent Affirmation before speaking |

| **TALKS:** | • **NEGOTIATING/ROLE PLAYING:** |

- Break down into groups of 4, one person for each scenario.

- In each group, "Joe" will go first and tell why he is so angry.

- Next, Alice speaks.

- Next, Supervisor speaks

- Evaluator leads his according to the questionnaire.

- Looking at "Be the Best That You Can Be" tips booklet, find tips that would be applicable to this situation.

- Review reasons why Joe is right.

- Review reasons why supervisor is right.

- Review reasons why Alice is right.

- How should this situation be handled? All of the scenes have occurred, now how can Joe be placated? Alice? Mrs. Jones? Is it possible?

- Each member of each group stands in place and tells his/her reaction to their assignment in terms of body language, attitude, human relation skills. Only one minute is required for each talk.

- Same procedure as before: clap for each presenter, talk, clap, comments from class, comment from instructor, write on cards.

**60 MIN.**

**ASSIGNMENT:** **NEXT WEEK: FAVORITE PERSON TALK**

Choose someone you admire and would like to talk about. The person could be a family member (parent, relative), a famous person (singer, actor), someone you have met and not met, someone you make up in your mind, an historical figure (Abe Lincoln), someone about whom you can tell a story. [Planning Sheet in Participant Packet.]

**SAMPLE TALK:**
- Instructor gives sample two-minute talk on Favorite Person.

**REMINDER:**
- Remember the importance of well-planned openings and closings.

## INSTRUCTOR NOTES: NEW INFORMATION TO BE WOVEN THROUGHOUT CLASS:

# AUDITORY: (38% of the message comes from the voice)

## VOICE RESEARCH:

- Generally speaking, if a person uses a great variety in pitch, we are likely to think of that person as dynamic and extroverted.

- Males who vary their speaking rate are viewed as extroverted and animated.

- Interestingly, females demonstrating the same variety in rate are perceived as extroverted, but also high-strung, inartistic, and uncooperative.

- If voice is flat, the person may be thought of as sluggish, cold, and withdrawn.

- A person with a nasal voice is often perceived as unattractive, lethargic, and foolish.

- Whether these perceptions are accurate or not, it's useful to know how people are likely to be perceived if they speak a certain way.

- Vocal cues can reflect attitudes, emotions, control, personality traits, background, or physical features. Our total reaction to others may be colored by our reaction to their vocal cues. from Richard Weaver II, <u>Understanding Interpersonal Communication, Fifth Edition</u>, Scott, Foresman/Little, Brown, Glenview, Illinois.

**EXAMPLE:**
- **"Close the door."** Say this statement from the following perspectives: a command, a plea, a request, a come on, a turn off.

**VOICE:** Refer to Student packets, "Voice." **(SEE ATTACHED)**

# VOICE

*[PACKET]*

If people perceive a discrepancy between what you say and how you say it, they will believe your voice. For example, if you see a tie you hate and say, "Nice tie, Joe," you could clearly be insulting his tie by your voice even though your words are complimentary. The following methods will help bring your voice and words into alignment:

- **BREATH CONTROL**: The more breath control you have, the more power your voice has. One way to learn to control how you breathe is to lie on a bed and put a book on your abdomen. If you are breathing correctly, the book should go up and down. (Remember our diaphragmatic breathing exercises.) To increase breathing control, take a deep breath, then exhale as you count to five. Repeat, increasing the count until you're exhaling to the count of 10.

- **VOLUME**: Read your audience's body language to determine if your volume is appropriate. If your voice is too loud, people will pull away or cross their arms as if to protect themselves. If your voice is too soft, your listeners will strain forward to hear you. Deliberately lower your voice to give importance to information or to exercise authority. When you lower your voice, you force your listeners to focus on what you are saying.

- **PITCH**: If your voice is too high, it will convey youth or nervousness. To find a comfortably low pitch, start speaking at a high pitch and count to 10, lowering your pitch with each count. When you find a pitch you like, practice speaking at that pitch until it automatically lowers to the new level.

- **HESITATION**: See sheet on "Toward More Powerful Speech." Usually hesitation is due to running out of breath. The solution is to take deeper breaths and release the air slowly so that it will last until you reach a natural place to pause.

- **PACE**: Speaking too fast indicates nervousness or being hurried or you don't want to be bothered. Makes you seem unapproachable. If you speak too slowly, listeners think you aren't sure of yourself or your information. Put more energy behind your voice, shorten pauses, and move quickly over vowel sounds.

- **ENUNCIATION**: Poor enunciation is usually the result of tension. Relax your facial muscles by yawning, tensing and relaxing your shoulder and neck muscles. Remember: your voice conveys messages that may hurt or help your image.

From Joan Sered Smith's (with P.A. Haddock) article, "Speak Up and Be Heard" in *Manager's Memo.*

- **RECOMMENDATION:** Use a conversational style of speaking. Speak to, not at, the audience as if you were speaking to a friend. Perfection is out. Reality is in. Allow the audience to "feel" that you, the speaker, are like them. Your goal is to establish rapport with your audience.

- **AVOID:** A monotone voice is deadly. Hypnotists use a monotone in order to relax a patient and enable the patient's mind to go blank. You don't want that. Raising your pitch, then lowering it will snap listeners out of their reverie. Speeding up, slowing down, and pausing are great ways to avoid the sleep-inducing monotone voice.

| | | |
|---|---|---|
| **PERCEPTION:** | • Describe the pitch of a dynamic/extroverted person. | |
| | • SHARE | **3 MIN.** |
| | • Describe person with flat pitch - sluggish, cold, withdrawn. | |
| | • Nasal - unattractive, lethargic, foolish. | **2 MIN.** |
| **VOCAL CUES:** | • Vocal cues reflect attitudes, emotions, control, personality traits, background or physical features. | |
| | • **CAN *THESE BE CHANGED?*** | **5 MIN.** |
| **PRACTICE:** | • "I didn't say he stole her money." Emphasize each word, one at a time. Seven words equals seven meanings. | |
| | • **POINT: It's how you say it that delivers the meaning.** | **3 MIN.** |

- "I'd love to go to dinner." Say four times, emphasizing the first, second, fourth, and sixth word. There are four different meanings according to the word emphasized. **2 MIN.**

- How many different ways can you say, **"Good Morning"? Try 10 different ways**. Go around the room and ask each participant to say the words, and ask them to use a different tone of voice than the previous person used.

  With each response, ask the class whether they would like to have breakfast with that person.

  This is a fun exercise that makes an obvious point. Change tone, pitch, inflection, emphasis on syllables, and you change the meaning of our words.

  Does it reflect what your mood and feelings are or should be, for the occasion? **10 MIN.**

**CONGRUENCE:** • Stress the importance of matching words, tone and body.

## MEANINGS IN CONTEXT:

- Put each of the following phrases on separate 3x5 cards:

  - "Get out of here."

  - "Come back."

  - "Are you busy?"

  - "What's that for?"

  - "Read it to me."

- Ask two volunteers to come forward; one will be the speaker, the other the listener.

- Volunteers: Study the list of phrases and imagine how they can be said differently to have different meanings. After listening to the phrase spoken by one of the volunteers, the class should determine:
  (1) The meaning of the message.
  (2) The intention of the message, judging by the tone. Was it intended to be playful or funny, authoritarian, dictatorial, pleading, helpful, judgmental, or other?
  (3) The implied relationship between the two people.

- Ask two more volunteers to come forward and read each phrase in a different tone of voice and ask the class to determine the meaning and the relationship between the speaker and listener.              **10 MIN.**

## MARK TWAIN STORY:

One day Mark Twain, who was known for his salty language was getting dressed. He went to his chifforobe and took out a shirt. It was missing a button, so he swore and threw it on the bed. As he was buttoning the second shirt, the button broke in half. Again, he swore and threw it on the bed. There was one shirt left. He put it on and as he was buttoning it, the button popped off. He took the shirt, slammed it on the bed and used every foul word he knew. What stopped his tirade was seeing his sweet, scowling wife standing in the doorway. She had heard every word.

In absolute disgust, she walked into the room, hands on her hips and decided to shock him. She repeated every foul word he had said. When she finished, she turned and saw him leaning up against the doorjamb with a twinkle in his eye.

He chuckled and said, "You got the words right, but you don't have the music."

- **POINT:** The tone, pitch, and volume of our words have more of a message than the words themselves.              **5 MIN.**

## WORD USAGE 7% of message:

- Ask class to "**describe a duck that is ready to eat.**" Half of the class will describe a yellow duck at a pond looking to find food. Whatever the majority of the class says, tell them they are wrong. What you meant was a nicely roasted duck, ready to eat for Thanksgiving.

  **POINT**: We don't all hear the same thing, even though the same words are used.              **5 MIN.**

*Gail A. Cassidy*

- Exchanging a bird for her husband: A husband buys his wife a parakeet for her birthday. His wife wanted a canary, so the next day she goes into the pet shop and asks if she return the parakeet for her husband. The shop owner replied, "We don't exchange pets for husbands." (*ha ha--a little levity.*)

**POINT**: Be aware of the words you use. People may hear what you don't mean.

**3 MIN.**

## TRY THIS:

**Match vocal cues with feelings perceived:**

| | |
|---|---|
| breathiness | affection |
| thinness | anger |
| flatness | boredom |
| nasality | cheerfulness |
| tenseness | impatience |
| throatiness | joy |
| increased rate | sadness |
| increased pitch variety | satisfaction |

**5 MIN.**

**QUOTE:**
- I know you believe you understand what you think I said, but I'm not sure that you realize that what you heard is not what I meant." -unknown. "You can observe a lot by just watching." -Yogi Berra,

**2 MIN.**

# TESTIMONIALS RELATING TO INCREASED CONFIDENCE

- "I've seen numerous changes in people's confidence levels in front of the class and have seen them improve drastically."

- "I was totally intimidated by all the seniors and thought I wasn't able to continue to take that class. But, as time went by, and with the help of the class . . . I was able to overcome the fear I had of speaking in front of the class. By the end of the semester I was able to stand up in front of the class in a confident manner and express myself.

  Effective Speaking has changed me in many ways. I am now able to raise my hand in class and not get nervous or turn red, because I have found my level of comfort. I truly believe that it was Effective Speaking which changed me. I am glad that I chose to stay in the class. Many of the participants showed drastic changes in the way that they speak. Everyone in the class has the ability to control an audience. Most of the participants in the class speak well, most participants will find that they can, in fact, go into a profession where there is speaking involved."

- "This was a class that I enjoyed very much, and at the same time learned even more. This class helped me with one of my biggest weaknesses and made me stronger in it than I ever thought I could be. I loved going to this class to see what I was going to learn that day. Plus, on top of everything else I believe that this class gave me a lot of self-confidence in myself that I never knew existed before."

# WEEK FOUR

## FAVORITE PERSON TALK

## TIPS FOR THE WEEK:

10 • Know that a person with high self-esteem does not need to find fault with others.

11 • Remind participants that people find fault with others when they feel threatened, consciously or unconsciously.

12 • Know that self-esteem is not noisy conceit. Self-esteem is a quiet sense of self-respect, a feeling of self-worth. Conceit is whitewash to cover low self-esteem.

ØØØØØØØØØØ

**OBJECTIVES:**
- To reinforce ways to relieve nervousness

- To learn the importance of listening

- To learn what causes poor listening

- To understand the basics of human nature

- To understand the importance of taking time to understand before being understood

- To tie together the entire communication package from Week One

- To understand how to relate well to an audience

- To learn Guidelines for preparing talks

**REVIEW:**
- Discuss significance of use of voice and words

|  |  |
|---|---|
|  | • What have they noticed as a result of studying body language, voice, and words? |
| **INSTRUCTOR:** | • See "Relate to Your Audience" sheet in packet (SEE ATTACHED)--discuss and answer questions. |
| **INSTRUCTOR:** | • Review "Guidelines" in packet. (SEE ATTACHED) |
| **WARM-UP:** | • Choose warm-up from Nervousness sheet and have participants practice. |
| **RAP TIME:** | • Pair off and practice |
| **AFFIRMATIONS:** | • Repeat your positive affirmations before speaking |
| **TALKS:** | • **FAVORITE PERSON TALK** |
|  | • **Same procedure as before: 1) Announce speaker, 2) Clap, 3) Talk, 4) Comments from class, 5) Comment from instructor, 6) Clap, 7) Write on cards.** |
| **ASSIGNMENT:** | **NEXT SESSION: 3-minute talk on WHAT I KNOW TO BE TRUE. Notice the addition of one minute to your talk.** **Examples:** Ask participants what experiences they have had that taught them a lesson and, as a result, can now say they knew this to be true, e.g., "Everyone needs to feel important." Now tell a story where you found how important it is to feel important. USE THE TIPS BOOKLET to find general statements, then recall a story which validates the statement. |
| **SAMPLE TALK:** | • Instructor gives sample **three-minute talk**. |

**(SEE SAMPLE PLANNING SHEET)**

*Gail A. Cassidy*

# RELATE TO YOUR AUDIENCE

## [PACKET]

- Speak with warm eyes.

- Tell your audience something special about them.

- Be humble!

- Use the pronoun "we" rather than "you."

- Whenever appropriate, mention the names of <u>some</u> of your listeners. The rest of the audience will pay even closer attention.

- Enjoy giving your talk.

- Be yourself. Avoid jokes if you are not a naturally funny person.

- Be sincere.

- Talk in terms of your audience's interests.

- Make sure your body language is congruent with your message. Remember:

  55% of all messages comes from your body, 38% from your voice.

- Know that you cannot **not** communicate.

- Smile.

- Communicate your genuine enthusiasm through your body and voice.

- Speak with a warm heart.

# GUIDELINES

- **NOTE CARDS**: Use 5x8 inch cards or 3x5 inch cards (if you want to keep them in your pocket) or an 8 1/2 x 11 inch sheet of paper folded lengthwise. Number your cards or pages in case you drop them.

- Do not write out your talks.

- Never memorize a talk word-for-word.

- Have an opening that will grab your audience's attention.

- Use evidence to substantiate your points.

- Know your subject thoroughly.

- **PRACTICE. PRACTICE. PRACTICE. Don't try to "wing" it.**

- Use visual aids when appropriate

- Close strongly so that the audience will be left with a strong impression of your talk.

- **Control "butterflies" by using**

  - Isometrics

  - Diaphragmatic breathing

  - Deep breaths to enable you to relax and visualize

  - Affirmations to psyche yourself.

*Gail A. Cassidy*

NAME:_____ DATE: _____

# PLANNING SHEET FOR PRESENTATIONS
## *[PACKET]*

**YOUR PURPOSE IN MAKING THIS PRESENTATION:**_____

_____

**OPENING: (Use exact wording)** _____

_____

**POINT #1:** _____

    **EVIDENCE:** _____

_____

**POINT #2:** _____

    **EVIDENCE:** _____

_____

(you may only have one type of evidence, such as a story, for a two-minute talk)

**POINT #3:** _____

    **EVIDENCE:** _____

_____

**POINT #4:** _____

    **EVIDENCE:** _____

_____

**CLOSE: (Use exact wording)** _____

_____

**MORAL:** _____

**BENEFIT TO LISTENERS:** _____

# LISTENING

**STUDY:** Ralph Nicols, University of Minnesota, tested thousands of participants and hundreds of business and professional people regarding *listening*. His conclusions are as follows:

- Immediately after people have listened to someone talk, they remember only about half of what they heard - no matter how hard they thought they were listening.

- University of Minnesota studies, confirmed by studies at Florida State and Michigan State, showed that two months later people will only remember 25% of what was said. In fact, people tend to forget 1/3 to 1/2 of what they hear within eight hours. **3 MIN.**

**CAUSES:**
- Causes of poor listening: Often deliberately tuning someone out because you don't like the person or because you are bored or simply tired.

- Listening is not a natural process. Why people tune out: the average rate of speech is 125 words per minutes. Human brain can process about 500 w/p/m. This means that your brain works with hundreds of words in addition to those you hear.

**EXAMPLE:**
- Ask the class if there is anyone who has thought about something other than what we are covering during this period--things such as someone you might meet in the hallway, something you plan to do after class, the next session, test, instructor, what you are going to have for dinner, etc. Of course you have. That is because you have a lot of time between 125 wpm being spoken and your ability to listen.

## HOW CAN YOU KEEP PEOPLE'S ATTENTION?

- Vary pitch, tone, speed, volume

- Be enthusiastic

- Engage your audience

*Gail A. Cassidy*

- Communication is a two-way street. To communicate we must express our ideas, our thoughts, and our feelings to others AND we must allow them to express their ideas, thoughts, and feelings to us.

## HEARING VS. LISTENING:

- Kevin J. Murphy in *Effective Listening*, wrote "Hearing and listening are not the same. Hearing is when your ears pick up syllables, words and sentences. Listening is the ability to categorize and process whatever you hear and draw conclusions."

**TO IMPROVE:** • To improve your listening skills, you must learn to be attentive, practice listening, concentrate on the important parts of what the speaker is saying. At the same time don't interrupt.**5 MIN.**

## IMPORTANT FACTORS TO REMEMBER:

1 **HUMAN NATURE:**

    A. No one likes to be wrong.
    B. Everyone wants to be appreciated.

2. Take time to understand rather than be understood.

- **Optometrist story:** One day a man went to visit his optometrist, saying he couldn't see well. The doctor took off his glasses and handed them to his patient. "These have worked for me for the past twenty-five years." The man still couldn't see.

**POINT:** What is good for one person is not necessary good for another. Try to understand before you are understood. *Seven Habits of Highly Effective People, Stephen Covey

**5 MIN.**

**Serenity Prayer:** • God, grant me the serenity to accept the things I cannot change, courage to change the things I can, and the wisdom to know the difference.

**PRACTICE:** • List things you cannot change.

- List things you can change

- Discuss difference     **10 MIN.**

- **Lighthouse Story** **4 MIN.**

Two battleships assigned to the training squadron had been at sea on maneuvers in heavy weather for several days. I was serving on the lead battleship and was on watch on the bridge as night fell. The visibility was poor with patchy fog, so the captain remained on the bridge keeping an eye on all activities.

Shortly after dark, the lookout on the wing of the bridge reported, "Light, bearing on the starboard bow."

"Is it steady or moving astern?" the captain called out.

Lookout replied, "Steady, captain," which meant we were on a dangerous collision course with that ship.

The captain then called to the signal man, "Signal that ship: We are on a collision course, advise you change course 20 degrees."

Back came a signal, "Advisable for you to change course 20 degrees."

The captain said, "Send, I'm a captain, change course 20 degrees,"

"I'm seaman second class," came the reply. "You had better change course 20 degrees."

By that time, the captain was furious. He spat out, "Send, I'm a battleship. Change course 20 degree."

Back came the flashing light, "I'm a lighthouse."

We changed course.

from Stephen Covey's *Seven Habits of Highly Successful People.*

### 3. **HUMAN RELATIONS STACK** [PACKET]

"Stacking" is a great mnemonic device to use to remember items, names, dates, or points in a talk. Once you know the points you want to make, you then develop them into a picture. For example, if you wanted to remember 9 human relations principles, you could picture the following: (The items underlined are those you want to have the participants clearly see.)

In your mind's eye, picture an ice statue of a cheerleader with headphones on. Look closely and you'll see, as in a cartoon, bubbles coming out of her head,

*Gail A. Cassidy*

indicating she is thinking. What she is thinking about is a <u>thermostat</u>, so she won't melt. In her <u>praying hands</u> is a huge <u>candy bar</u>. On the wrapper of the candy bar is a big <u>C</u> and a <u>plus sign</u> (<u>+</u>).

The pictures are explained as follows:

**<u>Ice Statue</u>:** Accept people as they are.

**<u>Cheerleader</u>:** Be enthusiastic in all you do.

**<u>Headphones</u>:** Listen. It is the greatest compliment you can pay someone.

**<u>Bubbles</u>:** Thoughts. Change your thoughts and you change your world. -Emerson.

**<u>Thermostat</u>:** You can't control what happens to you, but you can always control your reactions.

**<u>Praying hands</u>:** Accept what is, e.g., Serenity Prayer.

**<u>Candy bar</u>:** Treat others as you wish to be treated.

**<u>C</u>:** Do not criticize other people. No one ever appreciates it.

**<u>+ sign</u>:** Look for the positives in everyone.                    **10 MIN.**

**REMEMBER:**   •   If you always do what you've always done, you'll always get what you've always got.

## LONG-RANGE ASSIGNMENT: WEEK 12:

- In Part II of the Student's Manual, there is a section entitled "*Be the Best That You Can Be*," a guide to living well with others and being able to be the best that you can be.

- Using one of the principles in the booklet, talk on improving your relationship with someone you see on a regular basis.

- Review this section with students and have them choose one of the tips they feel they need to work on.

- Use regular Planning Sheet from your packets

- Complete Tips Talk Commitment Sheet

**(SEE ATTACHED)**

NAME:_____ DATE: _____

# TIPS TALK COMMITMENT SHEET
## *[PACKET]*

**(Choose one of the principles in the Tips booklet
to apply to the person of your choice.)**

**TIP CHOSEN:** _____

_____

**WHY DID YOU CHOOSE THIS TIP?** _____

_____

**PERSON WITH WHOM YOU EXPECT TO USE TIP:** _____

_____

**ON WHAT SITUATION DO YOU THINK YOU CAN USE THIS TIP?**

_____

**WHAT DO YOU HOPE WILL HAPPEN?** _____

_____

**WHAT WILL YOU DO IF THE TIP DOES NOT WORK THE FIRST TIME?**

_____

**HOW MANY TIMES WILL YOU ATTEMPT TO USE THIS TIP?**_____

_____

**PLEASE NOTE: The result of this Commitment will be reported in WEEK 12.**

_____

*Gail A. Cassidy*

ØØØØØØØØØ

# TESTIMONIALS RELATED TO
# <u>UNDERSTANDING OTHERS</u>

- "One of the major things about this course was not only talking to the class but listening to my classmates' presentations. Each person was unique in their approach."

- ". . . public speaking is more than an academic class, but a bonding class where people learn about one another by communicating."

- "Not only did I learn things for myself by actually getting up in front of a group, but I learned a good deal by watching and listening to others in the class."

- "Effective Speaking has also taught me how to listen to others and be able to pick out the positives."

- "Effective Speaking has helped me most with my people skills and conversational skills. I now listen better to what people say and do when they speak."

- "I got a lot out of Effective Speaking because I never knew how much I could affect so many people just by my preparation and the way I presented my stories. The thing I enjoyed the most is the positive feedback that I got from my fellow classmates.

  Because of the positive responses [the instructor] made the class comment on about each individual, the audience could see a complete metamorphosis in some participants--participants who were shy and did not have the comfort level that they had at the end of the year."

- "The reason I feel that this class is so effective to its participants is because it makes you listen to someone who maybe you have never spoken to before. It [the talks] will show sides of people that you probably think were never there. It also brings participants closer together; it gives a quiet person the spotlight for just 2 minutes and it also gives the normally loud 2 minutes to be serious as C. C. showed with his talk on his father. Just by that one talk I learned a lot about all the people in the class. No one said one word or laughed once because everyone knew it was time to be serious. To see that side of someone whom I thought would never be like that in front of a class, to see how he felt good after his talk, to get some of that off his chest, to feel better about one's self was worth taking this class."

- "I learned to respect others and realized that not everyone feels as comfortable as I do and that the best compliment I could give them was my full attention. I watched my peers improve and felt good about myself for being a part of it and proud of them for accomplishing their goals. I closely listened to the talks of the others in the class and learned a valuable lesson from all of them. Also, I learned that I can show many different sides of my personality and that people will still appreciate what I have to say."

# WEEK FIVE

## "WHAT I KNOW TO BE TRUE" TALK

## <u>TIPS FOR THE WEEK</u>

13 • Learn the Serenity Prayer: "God, grant me the serenity to accept the things I cannot change, courage to change the things I can and the wisdom to know the difference."

14 • "See" and/or "feel" your positive day before it actually starts. Use positive self-talk.

15 • Be (or act) enthusiastic about everything you do. It's contagious; it carries over to everyone you meet.

Ø Ø Ø Ø Ø Ø Ø Ø Ø Ø

**OBJECTIVES:**
- To reinforce ways to relieve nervousness

- To learn how to think on their feet

- To learn to be more precise in informing people

- To recognize the value of looking for positives

- To learn how to become a good storyteller

- To learn the importance of good enunciation

- To learn the importance of pacing

**REVIEW:**
- Discuss significance of human relations stack

- How can you use stacking in other places in your life?

**NEW MATERIAL:**    **REVIEW PACKET PAGES "ENUNCIATION" AND "PACING"**

| **WARM-UP:** | • Choose warm-up from Nervousness sheet and have participants practice. |

| **ASSIGNMENT:** | **NEXT WEEK: STORYTELLING** Come prepared to tell a **two-minute story and** a brief appropriate **joke**. |

**EXAMPLE OF JOKE:** Subject: A Dog Named Mace

A mechanic who worked out of his home had a dog named Mace. Mace had a bad habit of eating all the grass in the mechanic's lawn, so the mechanic had to keep Mace inside. The grass eventually became overgrown.

One day the mechanic was working on a car in his backyard and dropped his wrench, losing it in the tall grass. He couldn't find it for the life of him, so decided to call it a day.

That night Mace escaped from the house and ate all the grass in the backyard. The next morning the mechanic went outside and saw his wrench glinting in the sunlight. Realizing what had happened he looked up to he heavens and proclaimed.

"A grazing Mace, how sweet the hound, that saved a wrench for me!"

## INSTRUCTOR NOTES: THE HOW AND WHY OF STORYTELLING:
from *The How-To of Great Speaking* by Hal Persons.

• Jokes and plays have these elements in common: the setup, the crisis, and the payoff. This structure can be compared to a television commercials, where the elements are called *the grabber, the rationale,* and *the call for action* (you want the audience to laugh, buy, or applaud).

Jokes are a form of folk tale. Please don't memorize. Familiarize yourself with the gist of the story and tell it in your own words. For best results, personalize and localize your joke. Tell it about yourself, your family, or mutual acquaintances, using your locality or school.

## MORE BACKGROUND INFORMATION FOR STORYTELLING:

• The actor Michael Caine wrote a book, *Acting in Film*, where he stresses the use of eyes. "When you are the on-camera actor in a close-up, never shift your focus from one eye to the other. Sounds odd, doesn't it? But when you look at something, one of eyes leads. So during a close-up, be especially careful not to change whichever eye you are leading with. . . And I don't blink. Blinking makes your character seem weak. . . I emphasize the eyes because that's where it all happens."

*Gail A. Cassidy*

# ENTHUSIASM
## [PACKET]

Tom Peters said "Forget all the conventional 'rules' but one. There is one golden rule: Stick to topics you deeply care about and do not keep your passion buttoned inside your vest. An audience's biggest turn on is the speaker's obvious enthusiasm. If you're lukewarm about the issue, forget it!"

Think of someone in your life whom you really admire, someone about whom you could say, "Now that's a real winner!" First, if you know this person personally, you will probably be able to say that this person also makes you feel good. We tend to admire those who make us feel special.

Who is this person? Is it one or both of your parents, a relative, an instructor, coach, or friend?

Why do you admire this person? What qualities does he have? Is she "energetic?" Is "positive" a word you would use? How about "loyal," "respected," "giving," "honest," "courageous," "kind?" And how about "enthusiastic?"

Let's take a look at these descriptive words. First of all, many of the words relate to values. Secondly, notice whether these descriptors are skills or attitudes? Most definitely they are attitudes, and there is no school that I know of that offers a course in attitude. Perhaps there should be.

The importance of attitude was discovered through a research study done by the Carnegie Foundation for the Advancement of Teaching and later substantiated by additional studies made at the Carnegie Institute of Technology. The findings of these studies revealed that even in technical professions about 15 percent of a person's financial success is due to his or her technical knowledge and about 85 percent is due to their people skills - to personality and attitude, e.g., 15 percent for aptitude; 85% for attitude! How true the old saw, "It's your attitude, not your aptitude, that determines your altitude."

How can you change your attitude? Decide to. As I've said before, "Fake it until you make it." Act and you will be.

Enthusiasm is an attitude. An attitude is a thought. And it's exciting to know that we can control our thoughts all day long, therefore, our attitudes, therefore, our level of enthusiasm. It's all there for the thought!

# ENUNCIATION
## *[PACKET]*

A good voice commands respect and helps in holding your listeners' attention. A variety in pitch and increases and decreases in volume are essential in being a good storyteller. Also vitally important is articulation. Poor articulation arises from lazy lips, stiff jaws, or a thick, clumsy tongue.

To practice good articulation, read aloud three times the following tongue twisters. Record yourself on a tape recorder so you can hear how you sound.

1. She sells seashells down by the seashore.

2. She saw six slim, sleek, slender saplings.

3. Rubber baby buggy bumpers.

4. A big black bear ate a big black bug.

5. Sam shipped six slippery, slimy eels in separate crates.

6. The sixth sheik's sixth sheep's sick.

7. The sharp, shrill shriek of the bat shatters the shadowy silence.

8. Two terrible, tedious, tiresome talkers took advantage of the debating team.

9. The seething sea ceaseth and thus the seething sea sufficeth us.

10. Limber Lena leaped laughingly after Lazy Lally.

from *Basic Oral Communication, Fifth Edition*, Glenn R. Capp/Carol C. Capp, G. Richard Capp, Jr. Prentice Hall, Englewood Cliffs, NJ, 1990

Practice the following nursery rhyme three times. First, speak softly and slowly, making sure you clearly enunciate every vowel and consonant, then progress louder and faster for the last two times.

> Mary had a little lamb,
> Its fleece was white as snow;
> And everywhere that Mary went,
> The lamb was sure to go.

*Gail A. Cassidy*

It followed her to school one day,
Which was against the rule;
It made the children laugh and play,
To see a lamb in school.

To perfect your enunciation of "th's", practice Theopholis Thistle.

## THEOPHOLIS THISTLE, THE THISTLE SIFTER

Theopholis Thistle, the thistle sifter, sifted a sieve of unsifted thistles. Where is the sieve of unsifted thistles that Theopholis Thistle, the thistle sifter sifted?

Theopholis is a fun exercise to memorize and repeat to others. Initially, it seems impossible to get the "th's" in place, but mastery is such a satisfying experience.

# PACING:

[Packet]

When giving a talk or telling a story, Patricia Fripp, Pd.D., http:.//www.fripp.com, offers some great ideas to sound more intelligent, powerful, polished, articulate, and confident.

**TO SOUND MORE INTELLIGENT**, speak just a bit slower to allow yourself to select your most appropriate vocabulary and to give the impression of thoughtfulness.

**TO SOUND MORE POWERFUL**, use short, simple declarative sentences. You say what you mean, and you mean what you say. Cut out any useless connectors, adjectives and adverbs, especially superlatives.

**TO SOUND MORE POLISHED**, never answer a question with a blunt "yes" or "no." Append a short phrase of clarification. For example, "No, I did not see it." "Yes, I know Mary."

**TO SOUND MORE ARTICULATE**, make a special effort to pronounce the final sound in a word and use its energy to carry over to the following word. Pay special attention to final 't' and 'ng.'

**TO SOUND MORE CONFIDENT**, carry your body up. Hold your head as if you had a crown on it. Don't let your arms and legs have side to side motion when you move. Keep your elbows and knees close to the mid-line of your body.

**SAMPLE TALK:**
- Instructor gives example of a short joke and a two-minute story.

- IDEAS: Look at _Chicken Soup_ books. Learn a story that you can relate to the class.

- No preparation sheet necessary, but brief notes may be used.

**RAP TIME:**
- Pair off and practice

**AFFIRMATIONS:**
- Repeat your positive Affirmations.

**TALKS:**
- **3-MINUTE TALK - "WHAT I KNOW TO BE TRUE"**

- **Same procedure as before: 1) Announce speaker, 2) Clap, 3) Talk, 4) Comments from class, 5) Comment from instructor, 6) Clap, 7) Write on cards.**

**CATCH-UP TIME:**
- After the assigned talks are completed, this week is a good time to catch up on any material not yet covered. Whenever there is free time, the perfect activity to cover is impromptu talks.

## INSTRUCTOR NOTES:

**INTRODUCE IMPROMPTU TALKS:** Mark Twain once quipped that it took him weeks to make a good impromptu speech. With enough practice, anyone can become better than average giving an impromptu talk.

# IMPROMPTU TOPICS

Compile a packet of 3x5 index cards, each card having a noun written in the center, e.g. "cup, paper, soda, table, etc." Any noun can be used on a card.

Look at the following topics and choose at least 50 of them to type (or print) on 3x5 cards, which are used repeatedly.

Participants will be chosen at random, asked to come to the front of the room, pick a card from the pack (without looking), then come up with a story about the word on the card.

In order to give the participant an opportunity to think for 10 seconds, tell the class what is expected of them also. Give a few examples of words they could get and ask how many could come up with a story. Each participant should be allowed at least 10 seconds to think. There is always something the instructor can review. Even though Mark Twain once quipped that it took him four weeks to make a good impromptu talk, we are going to practice with a 10 second preparation time.

Explain "Spanning." If, for example, a participant picks the word "plane" but has never been on one, she could say, "Although I've never been on a plane, I did have the opportunity to go on a motorboat this summer. . ." That's spanning.

## SAMPLE NOUNS

| | | | |
|---|---|---|---|
| book | chair | desk | trainer |
| Halloween | Easter | rocket | seaweed |
| car | boat | plane | train |
| college | girls | dresses | shoes |
| baseball | football | soccer | tennis |
| sick | song | school play | New York |
| pop star | music | drums | band |
| piano | flower | money | bone |
| dog | cat | lion | ape |
| zoo | lawyer | doctor | instructor |
| novels | short stories | magazines | dream |
| locket | notebook | games | TV |
| sunset | vacation | laundry room | kitchen |
| den | mountain | ocean | money |
| clock | watch | alarm | cake |

| cookies | computers | puppy | gymnast |
| photographer | sister | brother | dad |
| mom | aunt | uncle | grandma/pa |

In order to get more interesting topics, distribute 3x5 cards to participants and have them write a topic. There may be duplicates, and that is fine. Some topics may have to be weeded out.

## PROCEDURE:

- Call participant's name. **Clap.**

- Fan cards and have participant pick a card. (They may dispute the word they received, but they have to go with it; otherwise, you will have every participant disputing every card.)

- Talk for 10 seconds while participant thinks.

- Time for one minute. **Clap.**

- No writing on participant evaluation cards is necessary for this assignment. Participants usually greatly enjoy this segment.

- Use Impromptu Talks to fill in time when assigned talks are completed.

## <u>REMINDER</u> FOR WEEK 12:

- Make sure you are working on your talk on using one of the principles to improve your relationship with someone you see on a regular basis.

## COLLECT COMMITMENT SHEETS FOR WEEK 12

ØØØØØØØØØ

## TESTIMONIALS RELATED TO
## <u>FRIENDSHIP</u>

- ". . . the best thing I got out of this class were the friendships and connections I made. It wasn't so much at all what I learned in this class this year, but who I learned about and I guess in a small way that I may have been able to do for them."

- "Effective Speaking is more than a class to learn how to speak; it's a class to learn to get out of your comfort zone and let people know the real you."

- "Effective Speaking brought all of us closer as a class. Just by getting up and sharing personal stories, we saw a different side to each person."

- "The speeches my classmates gave helped me to get to know others better and created a bond on which friendships could build. It was an icebreaker to help spark new friends and acquaintances."

# WEEK SIX

## STORYTELLING

## TIPS FOR THE WEEK

16 • Accept participants as they are, and then provide the atmosphere for them to learn and love learning.

17 • Learn from every colleague, every participant.

18 • Ask yourself, "Does it really matter?"

ØØØØØØØØØ

**OBJECTIVES:** • To reinforce ways to relieve nervousness

• To learn importance of enthusiasm

• To learn how to tell a story well

• To learn app+ropriate timing and pausing

**REVIEW:** • Discuss impromptu talks

• What is the value of practicing impromptu talks? [Being able to think on your feet is its greatest value. Give examples of being at a party and joining in on a conversation or being in a class and having to think fast. This is an exercise in training your mind to work faster.]

## ASSIGNMENT FOR NEXT WEEK:
## TWO TALKS: SHOW AND TELL TALK and PET PEEVE TALK

## TALK #1:

1. **USE OF VISUALS** (one-minute talk) **No preparation sheet is necessary**

• Look for something you are particularly proud of: a trophy, an article in the paper about you or your dog or family member, a special pen you use, a special gift, an award of some sort--anything that you can use as a prop in your story next week.

- ## RULES FOR USING AN ITEM:

1. Use prop only when it comes up in your talk.

2. Hold prop steady. Don't move it to emphasize points.

3. Make sure it does not cover your face.

4. Make sure you look at the audience as you speak and not your prop.

5. When you are finished using the prop, place it aside so it does not distract from your talk.

- Make sure you have an incident in which the prop plays a part, e.g., the day the phone rang and you were told that your picture was going to be in the paper, the day you received your gift, the game you played to earn the trophy you have, something special that happened as you were making your project.

**SAMPLE TALK:** • Instructor gives a sample talk using an exhibit.

**TALK #2: 2. PET PEEVE TALK (something that annoys you.)**
          **(2 minutes)**

**SAMPLE TALK:** • Instructor gives example of a time when something happened that really annoyed him/her, e.g., getting in the wrong line at the supermarket, being cut off on the highway, being lied to, losing something important. The annoyance must be within a story that happened.

## INSTRUCTOR NOTES: POINTERS FOR STORYTELLING:

- Emphasize that enthusiasm is contagious. You want the audience to feel your enthusiasm when telling a story or trying to convince or sell them.

- How can you make yourself enthusiastic? Decide to. "Fake it until you make it." Act and you will be.

**CHARISMA:** There was a letter to "The Pinstriped Advisor," an Executive Edge newsletter, asking "What, if anything, can I do to be more charismatic? Or is charisma something you're born with and you either have it or you don't?"

Pinstriped Advisor had an excellent answer. He said, "Charisma is not a goal. It's a byproduct - of your passion and drive, of your commitment to ideas and people. It comes when you show courage and make sacrifices. It flows out of your caring and your honesty. Sure, these are old-fashioned words - but they're the qualities that make people devoted to you and willing to follow you.

"So, don't try to live somebody else's idea of charisma. Still, you can do things that will enhance your chances of being charismatic - or at least having influence over people. 'Probably the most important thing you can do is to make a conscious effort to be more enthusiastic,' says Philip H. Friedman, Ph.D., 'You'll notice that no matter the person, those whom we describe as charismatic are always enthusiastic. And it's their enthusiasm that affects people. So, when you wake up, tell yourself you will be more enthusiastic. Psyche yourself up, visualize it and make a commitment to it by reminding yourself of the benefits that charisma will bring you.'"

**ENTHUSIASM:** Enthusiasm is an attitude. An attitude is a thought. And it's exciting to know that we can control our thoughts all day long, therefore, our attitudes, therefore, our level of enthusiasm. It's all there for the thought! (SEE ATTACHED)

## HOW TO BE ENTHUSIASTIC: GREAT QUOTES

- "Act enthusiastic and you'll be enthusiastic." -Carnegie

- Mark Twain said he was born excited and that is the reason for his success.

- Napoleon Hill: "Enthusiasm guarantees your point will be positive."

- Thomas Edison: "When a man dies, if he has passed enthusiasm along to his children, he has left them an estate of incalculable value."

- Emerson: Nothing great was ever achieved without enthusiasm."

- Shakespeare: "Assume a virtue if you have it not."

- "Years wrinkle the skin; lack of enthusiasm wrinkles the soul."

**WARM-UP:** • Choose warm-up from Nervousness sheet and have participants practice.

**RAP TIME:** Pair off and practice. Use a different partner than you practiced with before.

**AFFIRMATIONS:**   •   Repeat your positive affirmations.

**TALKS:**   •   **2-MINUTE STORY, preceded by brief joke.**

   •   Speakers may sit on chair or stool in front of room and pretend they are addressing a group of youngsters.

   •   Emphasize facial expressions, pausing for dramatic effect, and looking carefully at each member of the audience.

   •   **Same procedure as before: 1) Announce speaker, 2) Clap, 3) Talk, 4) Comments from class, 5) Comment from instructor, 6) Clap, 7) Write on cards.**

# ENTHUSIASM
[PACKET]

Tom Peters said "Forget all the conventional 'rules' but one. There is one golden rule: Stick to topics you deeply care about and do not keep your passion buttoned inside your vest. An audience's biggest turn on is the speaker's obvious enthusiasm. If you're lukewarm about the issue, forget it!"

Think of someone in your life whom you really admire, someone about whom you could say, "Now that's a real winner!" First, if you know this person personally, you will probably be able to say that this person also makes you feel good. We tend to admire those who make us feel special.

Who is this person? Is it one or both of your parents, a relative, an instructor, coach, or friend?

Why do you admire this person? What qualities does he have? Is she "energetic?" Is "positive" a word you would use? How about "loyal," "respected," "giving," "honest," "courageous," "kind?" And how about "enthusiastic?"

Let's take a look at these descriptive words. First of all, many of the words relate to values. Secondly, notice whether these descriptors are skills or attitudes? Most definitely they are attitudes, and there is no school that I know of that offers a course in attitude. Perhaps there should be.

The importance of attitude was discovered through a research study done by the Carnegie Foundation for the Advancement of Teaching and later substantiated by additional studies made at the Carnegie Institute of Technology. The findings of these studies revealed that even in technical professions about 15 percent of a person's financial success is due to his or her technical knowledge and about 85 percent is due to their people skills - to personality and attitude, e.g., 15 percent for aptitude; 85% for attitude! How true the old saw, "It's your attitude, not your aptitude, that determines your altitude."

How can you change your attitude? Decide to. As I've said before, "Fake it until you make it." Act and you will be.

Enthusiasm is an attitude. An attitude is a thought. And it's exciting to know that we can control our thoughts all day long, therefore, our attitudes, therefore, our level of enthusiasm. It's all there for the thought!

**AWARENESS**: • Go through the following with participants to discuss each section with them.

# TOWARD MORE POWERFUL SPEECH
## [PACKET]

| SUGGESTIONS | EXAMPLES | COMMENTS |
|---|---|---|
| Avoid hesitations. | "I er want to say that ah this one is er the best, you know." | Hesitations make one sound unprepared and uncertain. |
| Avoid uncertainly expressions. | "Maybe we could perhaps go there later. I guess we should. I think that is it." | Uncertainly expressions communicate a lack of commitment, direction, and conviction. |
| Avoid over politeness. | "Excuse me, please, sir," | Over polite forms signal one's subordinate status. |
| Avoid too many intensifiers. | "Really, this was the greatest; it was truly phenomenal." | Too many intensifiers make one's speech all sound the same and do now allow for intensifying what should be emphasized. |
| Avoid simple one-word answers. | "Yes; no; Ok; sure." | One-word answers may signal a lack of communication skills and a lack of interest and commitment. |
| Avoid disqualifiers. | «I didn't read the entire article, but.; I didn't actually see the accident, but." | Disqualifiers signal a lack of competence. |
| Avoid disclaimers that express a lack of conviction or expertise. | "I'm probably wrong about this, but.; I don't know anything about taxes, but | Disclaimers deny responsibility for one's statements and may call into question their validity. |

*Gail A. Cassidy*

| | | |
|---|---|---|
| Avoid weak modifiers. | "This looks pretty good; I look this one, kind of." | Weak modifiers make one seem unsure and indefinite. |
| Avoid tag questions. | "That was a great movie, wasn't it?" "She's brilliant, don't you think?" | Weak modifiers need another's agreement and therefore signals one's need for agreement and one's own uncertainly. |
| Avoid self-critical statements. | "I'm not very good at this." "This is my first public speech." | Self-critical statements signal a lack of confidence and make public one's inadequacies. |
| Avoid clichés and "bromides." | "Tried and true." "Few and far between." "She's as pretty as a picture." | Clichés and bromides (phrases and sentences that have been worn out by too-frequent usage) signal a lack of originality and creativity and a reliance on stock phrases and sentences. |
| Avoid slang and vulgar expressions. | "##!!!///****; no problem!" | Slang and vulgarity signal low social class and hence little power. |

DeVito, Joseph A. <u>The Interpersonal Communication Book, Fifth Edition</u>. New York: Harper and Row, 1989.

**REMINDER FOR WEEK 12:** • Make sure you are working on your talk on using one of the Tips to improve your relationship with someone you see on a regular basis.

# TESTIMONIALS RELATED TO ACCEPTANCE

- "I, as well as every other student in this class, have grown as a speaker from the beginning to the end of the course. We have improved whether it was through our confidence, our articulation, or our whole demeanor in general.

  This class is very genuine because we the class have come together and bonded through sharing and listening to the speeches that we told. I enjoyed listening to the points and morals of some of the talks, which were very important for life's everyday lessons such as self-esteem, treating others with respect, and the deaths of loved ones. I gained the feeling that we have come together and bonded with each other all because of this class. Now, because of this class, I am comfortable with speaking in front of a large audience. Therefore, I'm very glad to have taken this class and I can contend that the title of this class is very fitting."

- "This class helped me open up a lot. I became a lot more comfortable with who I am. When I talked about my parent's divorce and then seeing the support of my class, their listening and their applause made me feel a whole lot better about my speech, my situation, and myself.

  I also learned not to judge people. Prior to this class, I thought DB, KG, and JR were all snobs, jock jerks, and conceited know-it-alls respectively. I found out they weren't and that they are probably some of the nicest people I go to school with. . . . through this class I learned not to think bad things about everyone else.

  Last December I went to Northeastern University for an interview and the interviewer asked which is your favorite class. Even though I get A's in history and English, I said that Effective Speaking was. It helped me open my shell and discover that showing people the real true me is a good thing and they will always like and respect it."

- "The reactions I got from the class was a good feeling. Their reactions made me stronger and gave me so much more confidence."

- "From Effective Speaking I have acquired a skill of patience. I have learned that it isn't that easy for someone to get up and do speeches. Because of this I give them my undivided attention and respected them when they make a mistake. I have also become more open with others in and from this class. I have made friends from this class, who encourage me outside of class to speak as I feel. I believe Effective Speaking is a course where you learn more about you as a person, which helps you relate to others."

*Gail A. Cassidy*

- "In this class people can be themselves and not worry about stupid comments or be made fun of because [the instructor] always keeps the class on a positive note."

- "The final and probably most important skill that I learned in class was to only look for the positive in people. Because we were instructed to write down only positive things on our evaluation cards, picking out the good in people instead of bad has become second nature to me. This skill not only makes other people feel better, but it also reflects itself on my own disposition. When a person learns to see the positive in other people it brings a much more peaceful, optimistic outlook to the rest of the world around them."

- "In the beginning I felt I was probably nervous because I did not know how everyone would react to my talks. Just the thought of having to go up and look at everyone made me nervous but once I heard the class's comments, I gradually started to relax. The class support definitely made the class less pressuring."

- "The encouragement I received from my classmates helped me through each speech. This class gave me the ability to get my thoughts and feelings to the audience."

- "...it helped me become stronger as a person by hearing all the positive things being said about me. .helped me grow out of my shyness."

# WEEK SEVEN

## SHOW AND TELL PET PEEVE

## TIPS FOR THE WEEK

19 • Being right does not always work, e.g.,
Here lies the body of William Jay, who died maintaining his right of way. He was right, dead right as he sped along, but he's just as dead as if he were wrong.

20 • **HAVE FUN!**

21 • Park your ego at the door; it hinders relationships with participants.

ØØØØØØØØØØ

**OBJECTIVES:**
- To reinforce ways to relieve nervousness

- To learn how to speak more powerfully

- To learn how to effectively convey feelings about an annoyance in one's life

- To learn how to "sell" an idea, product, concept

- To learn how to use a prop effectively

**REVIEW:**
- Discuss value of storytelling

- Where else can you use storytelling skills?

- What did you learn about yourself as a result of storytelling?

**NEXT WEEK'S TALK:** **SALES TALK (USE ATTACHED SALES PLANNING SHEET)**

**HOW TO:**
- Get examples from participants of products to sell.

- Discuss opening sentence, a question bearing on a need.

*Gail A. Cassidy*

- Clarify the benefits (not the features) for the audience of buying your product.

- What problems will your product solve?

- Why should they relate to your product?

## EXAMPLES OF OPENING LINES FOR SALES TALKS:

- **SELLING A COURSE IN DESIGNING YOUR LIFE:** If loving what you do every day and earning money are important to you, would you be interested in learning more about how this could be?"

- **SELLING A CELL PHONE:** "If you could have clear reception and unlimited minutes at an affordable price, would you be interested in learning more?"

- **SELLING A COMPUTER:** "If portability, reliability, and low cost are important computer needs for you, would be interested in learning more?"

- **TRAVEL AGENT:** "If your ideal vacation trip met your expectations at a low cost, would you be interested in learning more?"

- **SPEAKING COURSE:** «If there were a way for you to have the confidence to address a large audience, is that something you would like to hear more about?"

**WHAT'S IN IT FOR ME?** is the question that has to be answered in a sales presentation.

- People buy on emotion/feeling first, then logic.

- When appropriate, appeal to buyers' senses: touch, taste, feel, see, hear.

- Analyze TV commercials and magazine advertisements. How are they appealing to their audiences?

**SAMPLE TALK:**   Instructor gives sample sales talk.

NAME:_____ DATE: _____

*[PACKET]*

# SALES PRESENTATION
[USE BACK OF PAGE TO COMPLETE YOUR ANSWERS]
**PLEASE USE NOTE CARDS FOR YOUR ACTUAL PRESENTATION!!!**

**OPENING: First sentence will be question bearing on a need.**

- Question bearing on a need of the listener(s), e.g., "If there were a way for you to totally relax and enjoy a rainy day (or whatever two things your product will do for the listener), is that something you would like to hear more about?" Write your exact question with the two benefits for the reader: _____
_____

**ESTABLISH NEEDS**

- Why should listener(s) buy your product? What will it do for them?
- List **the benefits of buying your product** (or what the product will do for them):

1.
2.
3.
4.

**SOLUTION:**

- I would like to recommend [name of your product], because [use any of the reasons you have filled in listed below

**WHY?** List reasons why, e.g.,

1. What the product is and how buyer can relate to it:_____
_____

2. Why should they relate to product? _____
_____

3. What is significance of product? _____
_____

*Gail A. Cassidy*

4. What feature(s) of your product can they use? _____

5. How will your product help solve their problems?

6. What is most exciting/outstanding about this product for you?

Write a brief, yet very strong, summary of why a person should buy your product. Then ask for them to buy it.

## CLOSING SENTENCE:

**WARM-UP:**
- Choose warm-up from Nervousness sheet and have participants practice.

**RAP TIME:**
- Practice

**AFFIRMATIONS:**
- Positive self-talk

## THIS WEEK'S TALKS:

1. **One minute TALK WITH PROP.** Make sure you have a story.

2. **Two minute TALKS OF ANNOYANCE**

- Emphasize importance of congruence. Words must match facial features which must match body action.

- Pitch, volume, pace will indicate level of annoyance.

## EXTRA TIME IN WEEK: Impromptus

## REMINDER FOR WEEK 12:

- Make sure participants are working on their talk on using one of the Tips to improve their relationship with someone they see on a regular basis.

ØØØØØØØØØ

# TESTIMONIALS RELATED TO
# NERVOUSNESS

- "Upon finishing [my talk] I was pleasantly surprised and relieved that no one laughed, they just applauded. I faced my fear, got the courage to speak and I felt success for the first I spoke in front of a group. From that day forward I was able to face the crowd and speak."

- "With this course I mastered the technique of getting over my nervousness."

- "Now after taking the class I realize that being nervous is really just all in our heads."

- ". . . I found how to relax myself in front of people. Now it's easy to get in front of a class. I can just get right up and tell it [talk] without any hesitations. Everyone is there watching me and telling me that I did a wonderful job."

- "Taking this course has not only helped cure my nervousness and bring about unforgettable experiences, but it has also helped me to be a better person."

- "Interview with Rider University: "When I got to the interview I was a nervous wreck. I remembered the talk we had on nervousness. I used the finger technique to keep my poise. I think that is the main reason I got accepted to Rider."

- "My Effective Speaking class has given me the confidence, courage, and preparation skills to go up and speak--and do it well."

- "I feel that I have improved simply because I feel more comfortable up there and I know how to prepare for a talk.

  You really get to know people and what they are about. That is the definite value and it makes the class all that more special."

- "Just a few months ago, I would have shuddered at the thought of having to speak before an audience. I knew once I was up in front of the room, my stomach would be in a knot, my hands would be clammy, and my heart would be pounding out of my chest. I would be trembling all over, and my voice would convey my nervousness.

  However, now if I need to speak before an audience, I'm not overwhelmed by the sense of dread I had once felt before. The Effective Speaking class helped me to overcome my fear of public speaking. Although I might still feel a little nervous at times, I now know how to calm myself down by using breathing or other techniques, and I know how to appear comfortable and confident in front of an audience even if I feel it not. Also, stepping outside of my comfort zone helped me to see different ways to capture an audience's attention."

- "When I began this course in September, I was very nervous when presenting myself in front of the class. At this point in time, I do not feel that nervousness any longer. In fact, it has been amazing to watch as the people in my class have changed along the way and become so much more comfortable speaking in front of a large group of people. "People skills" are probably one of the most important tools that one needs to order to become successful. And it is true when they say that first impressions leave a lasting mark. So, I feel that this course has helped me to improve my "people skills," and in the long run, that will help me greatly.

    The Effective Speaking course offers participants something beyond the basics, and in that, helps each person progress into an eloquent and poised speaker. This is a skill that comes into play every day and is essential to the success of each person. In my own personal experience with this course, I feel as though I have transformed from someone who might come across shy to a very articulate speaker who is now comfortable when speaking in front of an audience. Effective Speaking may not be a course that helps you get a 1600 on the SAT's, and its influence on the student may be more subtle, but in the long run Effective Speaking is remarkably "effective."

- "I am happy that I have taken this effective speaking class. I'm fortunate that it was offered as an elective because of the countless ways that it has helped me right now and for the long run. This class was a great learning experience. At the start of the course I nervously approached the podium and struggled to speak in front of my peers. However, I shouldn't have been uneasy because [the instructor] does not allow anyone in the class to snicker, mock, or laugh at the speaker. Also, after each speech we compliment the speaker with only positive feedback. In a world where we constantly hear negatives, it is nice to receive positive regards from others because by doing so it helps increase our self-esteem. The class has always been respectful to one another, and the value of respect has always been enforced and upheld in Effective Speaking."

- "...this class helped me a lot. I am a very shy and quiet person. And what I learned in Effective Speaking got me to be more sociable and to not be so nervous in front of people in any kind of situation, may it be just talking to someone or talking in front of a class. This class has helped me a lot. And also when in the class you get to see what other people think and feel are your strong points, it makes you feel better. So, you know people don't have it in for you if you are the paranoid type."

# WEEK EIGHT

## SALES PRESENTATIONS

## <u>TIPS FOR THE WEEK</u>

22 • Give participants a reason to check their negative attitudes at the door also.

23 • Know that participants "mirror" you. They reflect what they see, hear, and feel from you.

24 • Shake things up. Make changes. "If you always do what you have always done, you'll always get what you always got."

ØØØØØØØØØØ

**OBJECTIVES:**
- To reinforce ways to relieve nervousness

- To learn how to speak more powerfully

- To learn how to sell a product, idea, or concept

**REVIEW:**
- Discuss value of last week's talk on annoyance

- What is the value of practicing that type of talk?

**ASSIGNMENT:**
- **TWO-MINUTE TALK TO ENTERTAIN**

- Discuss what is considered entertainment

- Participants can work together for this assignment. Each participant is required to fulfill a two minute segment

- No preparation sheet necessary

- Find a play or story to tell the group.

- Notes may be used but no reading is allowed.

*Gail A. Cassidy*

**SAMPLE TALK:** • Instructor gives sample 2-minute talk to entertain.

**TODAY'S TALKS:** • **SALES PRESENTATION (2 minutes) Preparation sheet necessary.**

**REMINDER FOR WEEK 12:** • Make sure participants are working on their talks on using one of the Tips to improve their relationship with someone they see on a regular basis.

ØØØØØØØØØ

# TESTIMONIALS RELATED TO
# <u>SPEAKING SKILLS</u>

- "The spontaneous impromptus help me to get my mind flowing a bit quicker than usual."

- "Thinking on my feet is something I am walking away with."

- "A person cannot communicate well if he does not master the art of speaking, and I feel that I have definitely improved because of practice and good teaching.
  I always loved speaking in public, but I had one problem. I was nervous; I could not overcome my nerves. This class taught me ways to relax, and the constant speaking in front of the room method worked."

- "[The instructor] never told anyone to stop doing something. It was always how about trying it this way and when you're being told to try new things, you feel yourself changing for the better inside and out by your peers."

- "I learned so much. I learned about body gestures, different techniques to grab the audience's attention, ways to remember talks, and more importantly that I had what it takes to be an instructor."

- "I feel more confident and more relaxed in front of a group. My nervousness has dropped considerably, and I am not afraid to give a talk. Without this class I probably would have been just as nervous as I was before I took this class. I don't know if I need these speaking skills in college, but I am glad that I took this class and it was really worth it."

- "... watching and hearing other participants speak helps you to become a better speaker. Listening to others speak also helps to develop your listening skills."

- "It [Effective Speaking] has provided me with the skills necessary to deliver a dynamite talk to a large group."

- "We also learned to use these strengths to our benefit. Focusing on the positive played a significant part on my becoming more confident."

- "I saw how it greatly affected my fellow classmates. In one semester I saw people transform from shy and intimated to dynamite speakers. I did not just learn speaking techniques but the strength of the human spirit."

- "I feel the closest to our effective speaking class because we were able to get to know each other so well."

- "The main thing I liked about this class was it taught me how to remember my talks without memorizing it or reading it word for word from a piece of paper."

- "Most of all, I think this class has helped me organize my talk. I can go up to the front of a class, get a situation and speak about it. I can connect it in my life to a real experience. I can also improvise. I can make up a story so quick now. This class I consider to be one of the best courses in the school."

- "The most important thing we learned was how to plan a talk. For every talk I had to fill out a planning sheet. This helped me organize my talks and ensure that the talk had a beginning, middle and end. Having a specific format keeps the audience interested because it cuts down on rambling. The techniques for opening and closing a talk will always stick in my mind."

- "I learned that eye contact is a very important factor and including a personal incident helps to capture the audience's attention."

- "One of the ways I learned to capture the audience's attention was my silent pauses and my alert eye contact. It helped me so much. This was my favorite class."

- "This class helped me on being more creative and helped me making pauses (when my mind goes blank) look like part of my speech."

- "I used my new ability to be comfortable in front of a group to give a speech and in a presentation, I gave in one of my classes. Being able to enunciate my words enabled me to seem more professional in college and job interviews.

    I use the relaxing techniques to calm myself down before wrestling matches. They help me focus and to perform a lot better. I don't know where I would be without this course."

- "This course has done much more for me than I ever expected. It has not just made me a better speaker, but it has made me a better person overall. I now feel more confident in my skills to relate to other people on a daily basis. I would recommend this class to everyone because the lessons they will learn they will carry with them throughout their lives. I never would have thought that I would get this much from a class when I could talk a lot and there was no final exam."

- "This class also prepared me for college and my future. I feel I am one step ahead of everyone that attends college with me in the fall."

- "I have improved in being able to give oral presentations in other classes. It helps with job interviews too."

- "Not only have I benefited from this course when it comes to formal speeches, but it has helped me in my everyday life as well. I'm more aware of the way I come across to people I meet for the first time, such as an older relative I've never met before, and I'm much more confident in interviews, both for jobs and colleges.

    Effective Speaking has helped me to be more aware of the way I present myself, so I appear to be calm, confident, professional, and responsible. Because, after all, first impressions are everything."

# WEEK NINE

## TALK TO ENTERTAIN

## TIPS FOR THE WEEK

25 • Show participants through your own example what fun having a great attitude is.
26 • Be patient.
27 • Positive attitudes in class are catching.

### ☉☉☉☉☉☉☉☉☉☉

**OBJECTIVES:**

• To reinforce ways to relieve nervousness

• To learn how to speak more powerfully

• To learn how to give an entertaining talk

**REVIEW:**

• Discuss value of last week's talk on sales

• What is the value of practicing this type of talk?

• Where can you use techniques learned?

**NEXT WEEK:**

• **4-MINUTE TALK TO PERSUADE**

• **Use a variety of types of evidence**

• **Select a cause/issue you feel strongly about and persuade class to your way of thinking. (SEE ATTACHED)**

• **Complete Planning Sheet indicating forms of evidence to be used. (SEE ATTACHED)**

# CAUSES/ISSUES *[PACKET]*
## WOULD YOU FIGHT OR MARCH FOR ANY OF THESE?
### (Choose one issue you would like to talk about)

Environment: Pollution - air and water

Education - quality

Health Care system made mandatory

Children's right to divorce parents - rights

The Homeless - rights

Energy - solar/nuclear

The Justice System - Victim's rights

Veterans: pensions, hospitalization

Nutrition: labeling laws, banning sugar

Politics: balanced budget, honesty

Campaign reform

Youth - curfews/laws

Three strikes you're out law

Small Business Tax Reform

Churches/synagogues - separation church/state

Spirituality: freedom of new age thinking

Public Safety issues

Infant protection

Child Care regulations

Home Health Care disabled

Tourism protection

Space Exploration

Animal Care & rights: vivisection

Literacy eradication

Civil Rights Issues

Fashion industry rip-offs

Books: Censorship

Movies: Censorship

Sport figures' salaries

CEO salaries

Federal tax equality

State sales tax

Local property taxes for education

Broadcasting responsibilities

Community Development

Research methods

Family Issues

Media responsibilities/ sensationalism

Elderly: Medicare, S.S.

Discrimination: race, sex, age, etc.

Immigration: tighter regulations

Agriculture: pesticides

Parks & Recreation: overuse & abuse

Substance Abusers: Drunk drivers

Law: fairness of justice system today

School funding: equality rich/poor

Government bureaucracy

Political Fleecing of America

Road & Bridges repairs: dangers

Non-profit Agencies: gov't support

Censoring the Internet

Handicapped legislation

Human Development Programs

Megan's Law

Justice System: equality/fairness

Water Rights

Defense budget

Balanced budget

Unions

Gay rights

Sexuality Issues

Art censorship

Music lyrics: censorship/responsibility

Corporate Downsizing

Food contamination

Gun laws - The Brady Law

Construction laws

Air bags on passenger side

Real Estate development

Religion

Late term abortions

Cloning human beings

*Gail A. Cassidy*

| Women's Issues | War |
| Honesty among politicians | Civility |
| Human Relation Principles | Kindness |
| Loss of the Rain Forests | Sincerity |

**LIST OTHER CAUSES AND/OR ISSUES YOU FEEL STRONGLY ABOUT THAT YOU WOLD RATHER TALK ABOUT:**

List adapted from *The Path* by Laurie Beth Jones.

NAME:_____ DATE: _____

## PERSUASION TALK
(USE BACK OF PAGE TO COMPLETE YOUR ANSWERS)
**PLEASE USE NOTE CARDS FOR YOUR ACTUAL PRESENTATION!!!**

**OPENING: First sentence will be a statement or question to challenge your audience to your way of thinking.** _____

_____

## ESTABLISH REASONS:

- Why should listener(s) believe in your point of view? What will it do for them?
- List **the benefits of buying-in to your belief** (or what will it do for them):
1.
2.
3.
4.

## SOLUTION:

- I would like to recommend _____, because _____ (use any of the reasons you have filled in listed below) _____ **WHY?** List reasons why, e.g.,

    1. What your belief is and how listener can relate to it: _____

    _____

    2. Why should they relate to your belief? _____

    _____

    3. What is significance of your belief? _____

    _____

    4. How will your belief(s) help solve their problems? _____

    _____

    5. What is most exciting/outstanding about your beliefs for you? _____

    _____

*Gail A. Cassidy*

- Write a brief, yet very strong, summary of why a person should believe you. Then ask for them to agree with you.

---

**CLOSING SENTENCE:**

---

---

**EVIDENCE:**  • Review Evidence Sheet. Encourage participants to utilize at least three different types of evidence in their talks to persuade. A story is great, but this time add additional types of evidence.

ØØØØØØØØØ

## EVIDENCE REMINDER

### [PACKET]

**CITING AN EXPERT:** Quoting someone in authority.

**FACTS/STATISTICS:** Numbers, comparisons, percentages.

**PROPS:** A visual, picture, object, drawing, etc.

**ACTION:** Act out how something works

**METAPHORS:** Making a direct comparison. Relate to something to which audience can relate, i.e., *the car skidded the length of a football field.*

**STORIES:** A story about something that has happened to you or to someone you know.

There are different types of stories you can use:

- **Vignettes:** brief, descriptive incident or scene which can be told in a minute or so. Historical events, examples, case studies.

- **Life and death stories:** stories of great loss, hardship, or pain. Olympic athletes, cancer survivors, people who have overcome incredible odds tell their stories. These stories deal with life and death and can be used to teach a profound lesson.

- **Embarrassing moment story:** Funny stories which allow us to be funny. Use to humanize yourself so audience can identify with you.

- **News stories:** Current events that can be used to prove your point and which add to your credibility.

- **Personal stories:** Ordinary experiences that prove your point.

adapted from Doug Stevenson's *Never Be Boring Again!*

The personal story is particularly effective because people like to hear something personal about the speaker. Everyone loves gossip, and stories fall into that category. People remember stories and, as a result, can relate better to the point being made by the speaker.

## PEOPLE LOVE STORIES!!

| | |
|---|---|
| **SAMPLE TALK:** | • Instructor gives sample 4-minute talk to persuade. |
| **WARM-UP:** | • Choose warm-up from Nervousness sheet and have participants practice. |
| **RAP TIME:** | • Practice |
| **AFFIRMATIONS:** | • Repeat your positive affirmations. |
| **TALKS:** | • **TWO-MINUTE TALKS TO ENTERTAIN** |
| <u>**REMINDER**</u> **FOR WEEK 12:** | • Make sure participants are working on their talks on using one of the Tips to improve their relationship with someone they see on a regular basis. |

*Gail A. Cassidy*

# TESTIMONIALS RELATED TO
# GENERAL REACTIONS

- "Richard Nixon once wrote in one of his many books, *In the Arena*, that, "the written word, no matter how elegant, is different from the spoken word. It is often too sterile and lacks rhythm and punch that a speech needs. That can be corrected to an extent if the speaker works the language through aloud." (Nixon 243). The former President was an astute politician and known for his successfulness in public speaking. He encouraged all to work on their speaking ability for success throughout their life and as the quote states, public speaking must be practiced and worked on. I realized this and decided that maybe I should take the class, and it has been one of the greatest experiences of my high school career.

     It is not a class using huge textbooks or a calculator, but it is a class that gets results, which will help us in life, not only in high school. I mean with sincerity that public speaking has opened me up to others, and I will definitely seek to take some type of speaking course in college."

- "Overall, this class has been the most exciting and entertaining class that I took."

- "This class is fun because it gives us a chance to be creative which we don't get to be very often."

- "This was the best elective that I could have possibly taken and I'm really glad that I did."

- "I did not know what to expect when I walked into my first day of Effective Speaking. Even though I chose this class as part of my schedule, I felt really nervous about it. I pictured myself standing in front of the class, red in the face and shaking life a leaf. I was worried that I would not know what to say or forget my words and look like an idiot. But as I watched my classmates do their talks, and then doing my talk, I felt like a big weight was lifted off my shoulders. I was excited to go to class and listen to the interesting talks that my classmates did, and I became less and less nervous after every talk I made."

- "Well once I got into the class, I loved every minute of it. I loved getting up in front of the class because they are such great people that they are in no way rude or disrespectful and they help you feel more comfortable up there. Whenever you ask a question, they respond with enthusiasm just to help you along in any way they can."

# WEEK TEN

## 4-MINUTE TALK TO PERSUADE

## TIPS FOR THE WEEK

28 • Show respect to get respect.
29 • Know that attitude is a choice everyone makes every day.
30 • Explain that people cannot help what happens to them, but they are **always** in charge of their responses.

ØØØØØØØØØØ

**OBJECTIVES:**
- To reinforce ways to relieve nervousness

- To learn how to speak more powerfully

- To learn how to persuade others to your way of thinking

- To effectively use various forms of evidence in a talk

**REVIEW:**
- Discuss value of last week's entertainment talk

- What is the value of practicing these types of talk?

**NEXT WEEK:** **READING.**

- Mark your copy carefully. Have participants refer to "Reading" in their packets.

# READING
### [PACKET]

Using a pen, mark your copy with the following symbols so you can read effortlessly and with meaning when you address the class.

- For a brief pause, use a slash (/) between words.

- For a full stop, such as the end of a sentence, use an x (X).

- To indicate a group of words should be said in one breath, underline the words in one straight line.

- If certain individual words are to be emphasized or punched, double underline them to remind you as you are reading.

**PRACTICE THE FOLLOWING:**

Four score and seven years ago / our fathers brought forth on this continent/ a new nation,/conceived in Liberty,/ and dedicated to the proposition that all men are created equal.X

Now we are engaged in a great civil war,/ testing whether that nation,/ or any nation/ so conceived and so dedicated,/ can long endure.X We are met on a great battlefield of that war.X We have come to dedicate a portion of that field/ as a final resting-place/ for those/ who here/ gave their lives/ that that nation might live.X It is altogether fitting and proper/ that we should do this, etc.

- Select a serious type of paper to read. Find something from a newspaper, novel, or speech.

- Make sure it is a two-minute selection.

- **PURPOSE:** To be an effective reader, not a boring one.

- Use your voice well, enunciate clearly, and make your audience feel as if you are not reading, but rather speaking about a topic you know well.

- **BE DRAMATIC**

**WARM-UP:**    
- Choose warm-up from Nervousness sheet and have participants practice.

**RAP TIME:**     Practice

**AFFIRMATION:** • Repeat your positive affirmations.

**TALKS TO PERSUADE**:

- Have participants clarify types of evidence they used upon completion of their talks.

- Notice types used most frequently.

**REMINDER FOR WEEK 12:** • Make sure participants are working on their talks on using one of the Tips to improve their relationship with someone they see on a regular basis.

ØØØØØØØØØØ

# TESTIMONIALS RELATED TO
# GENERAL REACTIONS

- "Of all the courses that I have taken so far at [school] I definitely believe that Effective Speaking has been the best, "funniest," and most helpful one. I love the fact that the class is based on all positives. It is really wonderful to hear about the good things you did and how great your talk was. Hearing the positives boosts the confidence of the speaker and helps them become more relaxed."

- "Effective Speaking is one of the best courses/decisions I have ever made."

- "I loved this class because it was all hands on, no lecturing involved."

- "You have taught me that no matter how great you are, you can always become better. I also learned that you have to find what's special within you and then others will love you for who you are.

  I have come to realize that if I have just an ounce of confidence you can move mountains. Effective Speaking should be a required course because it opens up your heart to what the world has to offer."

- "This class by far was my favorite class and one of the most helpful for my future."

- "Who would have thought that I would have come out of my shell in front of a room the way I did. This class also helped me see a whole other side of people that I would normally just walk by and not even give a thought about. This was a real personal class to the fact that some of my classmates opened up to all of us and shared personal experiences. I learned how not to show the fact that I am nervous because if I do I would be eaten alive in a positive way."

# WEEK ELEVEN

## READING

## TIPS FOR THE WEEK

31 • Remember, there is a pause between stimulus and response. Choose your response carefully.

32 • Ask your participants why they are **choosing** to be unhappy, bored, tired, sad, happy.

33 • Know that attitude is the steering mechanism of the brain. Body language can lead to attitude.

ØØØØØØØØØ

**OBJECTIVES:** • To reinforce ways to relieve nervousness

• To learn how to speak more powerfully

• To learn how to use your voice effectively

• To understand the importance of marking a copy that is to be read to an audience

• To read effectively

**REVIEW:** • Discuss value of different types of evidence used in last week's talks

• What is the value of using different types of evidence?

**NEXT WEEK:** • Make sure participants are working on their talks on using one of the Tips to improve their relationship with someone they see on a regular basis.

• What happened?

- Was the outcome good?

- How often did you try?

- How difficult was it?

**REVIEW STACKING FROM WEEK FOUR:** (REMINDER, you were to have chosen one of the "Be the Best That You Can Be" Tips to use on someone you see regularly. Next week you will report on your commitment.)

## TIPS STACK

"Stacking" is a great mnemonic to remember items, names, dates, or points in a talk. Once you know the points you want to make, you then develop them into a picture. For example, if you wanted to remember 9 human relations principles, you could picture the following: (The items underlined are those you want to have the participants clearly see.)

In your mind's eye, picture an <u>ice statue</u> of a <u>cheerleader</u> with <u>headphones</u> on. Look closely and you'll see, as in a cartoon, <u>bubbles</u> coming out of her head, indicating she is thinking. What she is thinking about is a <u>thermostat</u> so she won't melt. In her <u>praying hands</u> is a huge <u>candy bar</u>. On the wrapper of the candy bar is a big <u>C</u> and a <u>plus sign</u> (<u>+</u>).

The pictures are explained as follows:

<u>Ice Statue</u>: Accept people as they are.

<u>Cheerleader</u>: Be enthusiastic in all you do.

<u>Headphones</u>: Listen. It is the greatest compliment you can pay someone.

<u>Bubbles</u>: Thoughts. "Change your thoughts and you change your world." -Emerson.

<u>Thermostat</u>: You can't control what happens to you, but you can always control your reactions.

<u>Praying hands</u>: Accept what is, e.g., Serenity Prayer.

<u>Candy bar</u>: Treat others as you wish to be treated.

<u>C</u>: Do not criticize other people. No one ever appreciates it.

<u>+ sign</u>: Look for the positives in everyone.

**SAMPLE TALK:**
- Instructor gives a talk, using an incident when he attempted to use one of the Tips with someone he sees regularly.

**WARM-UP:**
- Choose warm-up from Nervousness sheet and have participants practice.

**READING:**
- Have participants be aware of enunciation, breath control, pitch, speed, volume.

**AFFIRMATIONS:**
- Repeat your favorite affirmation(s) to yourself.

**EXTRA TIME:**
- Get caught up

- More impromptu talks

- Reinforce information regarding *attitude*.

- Review essentials of *body language*.

*Gail A. Cassidy*

∅∅∅∅∅∅∅∅∅∅

# TESTIMONIALS RELATED TO
# GENERAL REACTIONS

- "The class is not public speaking; it's effective speaking. This class affected my life sufficiently. I am no longer afraid of speaking in public. My goal is to become an officer in the United States Marine Corp. Because of the course, I have more confidence now than I had before."

- "Effective Speaking to me is one of the most important classes in our school."

- "This course was my favorite course throughout this year."

- "I think every student should have to take the class because it teaches you how to speak in front of a room and actually feel comfortable. It teaches you to be prepared and how to relate to the audience. It teaches you how to stand, speak, move, etc."

- "What does one learn in 12+ years of education? Ideally, one learns how to add, subtract, read, write, and other tidbits pertaining to science, history, etc. Something is missing. There is something that we take part in everyday of our lives, yet 12+ years of education refuses to recognize it. Of course, I am referring to the art of speaking. The spoken word is indeed one of the most beautiful artistic talents in this world. With words we can cause others to shed a tear of sadness, crack a smile of hope, or conduct themselves in whichever manner they choose to feel after hearing our words float out of our mouths."

# WEEK TWELVE

## TIPS TALK

## <u>TIPS FOR THE WEEK</u>

34 • Have participants practice changing their attitudes by sitting or standing straight, with their heads up, and a smile on their faces. It does work!

35 • Know that it is the attitude of our hearts and minds that shape who we are, how we live, and how we treat others.

36 • Help participants to recognize their specialness.

**OBJECTIVES:**
- To reinforce ways to relieve nervousness

- To learn how to speak more powerfully

- To learn how to understand before you are understood

- To increase participants' sensitivity to others

- To improve participants' relationships with others

**REVIEW:**
- Discuss value last week's reading exercise.

- Discuss the effect of articulation, pitch, volume, speed in reading material aloud.

**NEXT WEEK:**
- <u>ESSAY DUE</u> (if applicable): 5 paragraph, typed, double spaced. [Details in Participant Packets.] **WRITING ASSIGNMENT**

### ESSAY DUE NEXT WEEK

Please write a five-paragraph, typed, double spaced essay on the following topic:

### "Of what value was this Course to me?"

Please construct this in the same manner you have constructed your talks. See a Planning sheet for ideas.

*Gail A. Cassidy*

- Do not include a discussion of the trainer

- You may include recommendations for future changes in the seminar, if you desire.

- You may share your reactions about the change in a fellow classmate.

We use this information to improve and update the seminar. Thank you!

- **TOPIC**: **"Of What Value Was this Course to Me?"** Please construct this in the same manner you have constructed your talks. See a Planning sheet for ideas.

  - Do not include a discussion of the instructor

  - You may include recommendations for future changes in the course, if you desire.

  - You may share your reactions about the change in a fellow classmate.

| | |
|---|---|
| **WARM-UP:** | • Choose warm-up from Nervousness sheet and have participants practice. |
| **RAP TIME:** | Practice |
| **AFFIRMATIONS:** | • Psyche yourself up for your talk |
| **TALKS:** | • Impromptu discussion of essays. |
| | • Summary of course |
| **PREPARATION:** | • Review Packet information. |

ØØØØØØØØØØ

# TESTIMONIALS RELATED TO <ins>GENERAL REACTIONS</ins>

- "What I am trying to get at here, is that while math may play a part in 40% of the actions in our lives, talking is involved in 90% of the actions found in our day. Whether we are giving a speech, speaking with a friend, or even talking to ourselves, it is still there. It almost seems insane not to help mold something as important as the spoken word, which plays such a huge role in our lives, during our years of schooling. By this you are obviously avoiding a section of children that excel in the spoken word, which in turn does not allow their talents to grow.

  I know this, because I was one of those children. The reason I "was" one of them is because I happened to take the class known as Effective Speaking. This class gave me ideas and led me in the right direction on how to channel my abilities. The many little "knickknacks" that I have learned in that class proved their worth rather quickly.

  "I had to deliver a speech in front of a semi-large audience of perhaps 50 people or so. I went in with some butterflies in my stomach, but surprisingly calm. I delivered perhaps the best speech of my life, not that I would think so, but the compliments I received convinced me that this class is the reason for my success. Without it I would have gone in totally ignorant to the audience's needs. That night was perhaps my proudest moment, for not only was I given the honor to speak, but also proved that the faith they put in me was not a mistake on their part. I have Effective Speaking and [the instructor] to thank for my proud moment "in the sun.""

# WEEK THIRTEEN

## REVIEW

## TIPS FOR THE WEEK

37 • Success is feeling good about yourself every single day. That is attitude.

38 • Know and share with your participants that true power is knowing that you can control your attitude at all times.

39 • Treat every participant as if he or she were your friend's child.

ØØØØØØØØØØ

**OBJECTIVES:**
- To reinforce ways to relieve nervousness

- To learn how to speak more powerfully

- To learn value to others of this course

- To learn recommendations for improvement

- To improve participants' relationships with others

**REVIEW:**
- Discuss the value of last week's talk on using human relation principles.

- Discuss the effect of using the principles on a daily basis with everyone we meet.

**ESSAY DUE:**
- Discuss papers on "Of What Value Was this Speaking Class to Me?"

- How did the Planning Sheets affect your writing of this essay?

# REVIEW DISCUSSION:

1. What is attitude?
2. Why is it important?
3. How does it affect you?
4. Can you control attitude?
5. How?
6. Do you control your thoughts?
7. Do your feelings come from your thoughts?
8. Therefore, do you control your feelings? Explain.
9. What are three ways to reduce nervousness?
10. What is perception?
11. How does perception differ from reality?
12. How can you not **not** communicate?
13. Give examples of how people don't all see the same thing.
14. What does a handshake tell you about a person?
15. How can you achieve charisma?
16. What are the percentages in the three divisions of non verbal communication?
    - Visual
    - Auditory
    - Words
17. How many meanings are in the sentence, "I wasn't going to enter the car."
18. How fast do we talk?
19. How fast do we listen?
20. What causes poor listening?
21. What are two basics of human nature?
22. Write out the human relations stack and tell what each means.
23. What did you learn about storytelling, the delivery?
24. What is the value of impromptu talks?
25. What can you do to be a more powerful speaker?
26. List the rules for using a prop in your talk.
27. How do you start a sales presentation?
28. What must be included in a sales presentation?
29. What did you learn from giving a talk to entertain?
30. What must be included in a talk to persuade someone to your way of thinking?
31. How can you improve your reading aloud skills?
32. List six forms of evidence.
33. List 5 ways to relate to your audience.
34. Describe an AFFIRMATION and tell why it is important.
35. Of what value are AFFIRMATIONS and when should they be used?
36. What is one cause of poor articulation?

*Gail A. Cassidy*

37. Describe three ways to bring your voice and your message into sync.
38. What does talking too fast indicate to your audience?
39. What does a high-pitched voice tell an audience?
40. Describe one way to improve enunciation.

## FINAL TALKS NEXT WEEK:

- **Participants have a copy of requirements in their Packets**

**FINAL TALK:**   **TALK TO CONVINCE/PERSUADE**

**LENGTH:**   5-MINUTES

**TOPIC:**   **TALK TO PERSUADE**

**Choose a popular, appropriate issue of your choice and persuade class to your way of thinking**

## FINAL TALK

## POINT CRITERIA

- 10 points:   Planning sheet
- 10 points:   Evidence used (3 forms)
- 10 points:   Timing--must go 5 minutes
- 10 points:   Impact on audience
- 10 points:   Opening
- 10 points:   Closing
- 10 points:   Organization of Talk
- 10 points:   Animation/enthusiasm
- 20 points:   Fulfillment of weekly recommended improvements

**PROCEDURE:**   • **Your name will be called at random.**

- **You will give your talk.**

- **Instead of commenting on your talk, your peers will summarize on back of your card how you have done in course.**

- **Two minutes will separate talks so class can write.**

- **No comments will be made by anyone.**

*Gail A. Cassidy*

ØØØØØØØØØØ

# TESTIMONIALS RELATED TO
# GENERAL REACTIONS

- "I don't want to leave the class at all."

- "Effective Speaking is hands down the class that has had the most impact on me throughout high school. I could go on about how well my ability to speak has improved and how effective speaking is so important. Everybody already knows how important it is and how the class helps participants become more comfortable speaking in public. I would speak of something I noticed about how the class affected some of the kids I know.

  What I saw was the changes in people's personalities. Shy people who would barely speak loud enough for you to hear them were screaming in your face at the end of the course. Some of the most impersonal people were able to share some truly personal stories with the class. Also, one of the most "un-outgoing" person in our class has changed completely. The way I see it is she changed from the things that went on in the class. She was forced to get up in front of class and talk to everyone. So this class may not be the most challenging or have the most work, but I feel that it's had the most impact on me and many of the other participants."

# WEEK FOURTEEN

# <u>FINAL TALK</u>

## <u>TIPS FOR THE WEEK</u>

40 • Never talk down to anyone.
41 • Find what is special about every participant.
42 • **SMILE**. It warms a classroom.

øøøøøøøøø

**OBJECTIVES:**
- To judge effectiveness of the course

- To determine what has been learned

**PROCEDURE:**
- Your name will be called at random.

- You will give your talk.

- Instead of commenting on your talk, your classmates will summarize on back of your card how you have done in course.

- Two minutes will separate talks so class can write.

- No comments will be made by anyone.

**CARDS:** **Collect cards from all participants after they have written their final comments.**

**LAST DAY:**
- Distribute collated cards to their originator.

- Have participants read the input from their peers.

- Discuss what they have read and how they feel.

## FINAL COMMENTS BY INSTRUCTOR

# APPENDIX

*Gail A. Cassidy*

*Gail A. Cassidy*

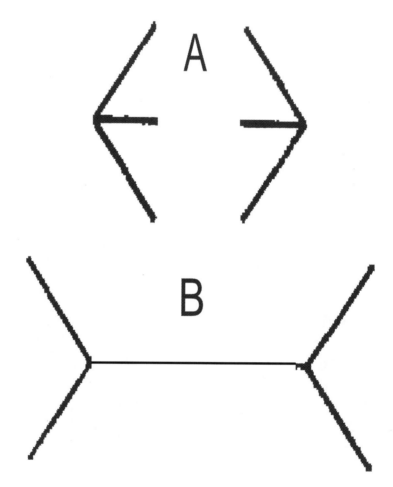

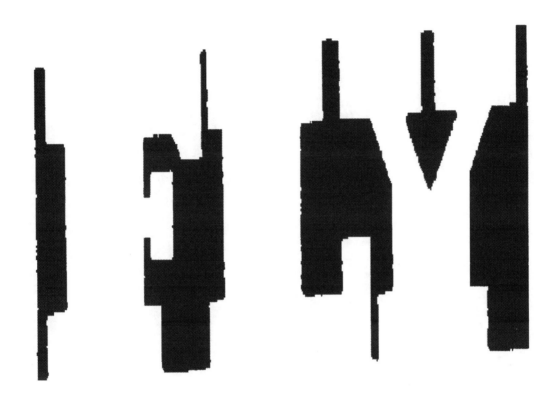

An excellent source for additional pictures is

<u>Can You Believe Your Eyes</u>? by J. Richard Block and Harold Yuker (Brunner/Mazel) 1992.

*Gail A. Cassidy*

# REFERENCES

## BOOKS ON SPEAKING AND IMAGING

Ailes, Roger. You Are the Message: Secrets of the Master Communicators. Illinois: Dow Jones-Irwin.
This book is excellent. I've used much of this material in programs I've developed. He gets into body language, intonation, etc. and gives excellent examples to prove his point.

Berg, Karen and Andrew Gilman. Get to the Point. New York: Bantam Books.
Authors are communication experts who work with AT&T and Chase Bank. They help speakers combat presentation anxiety, build a strong message, and create a polished style of delivery. Has some good information.

Caine, Michael. Acting in Film. New York: Applause Theatre Book Publishers.
I had to buy this after seeing Michael Caine interviewed one Sunday morning. The only thing of significance relating to speaking is the value of eye expression. Interesting but not worth buying.

Carnegie, Dale. The Quick and Easy Way to Effective Speaking. New York: Dale Carnegie & Assoc. 1962. Easy, elementary, and excellent information.

Decker, Bert. You've Got To Be Believed To Be Heard. New York: St. Martin's Press.
Interesting and worthwhile. He talks about importance of personal impact, truly persuading other people to listen to your message, learning to win their emotional trust before any effective verbal communication can take place.

Ehrlich, Eugene & Gene Hawes. Speak for Success. New York: Bantam.
Contains five keys to mastering successful speech, how to craft and deliver an effective written speech, how to make humor and visual aids work for you, how body language and eye contact enhance the power of a sales pitch, the fundamentals of voice preparation, enunciation and projection, how to improve diction and vocabulary and the 100 most common incorrect phrases to avoid--even a section on parliamentary procedure. .

Elgin, Suzette Haden. The Gentle Art of Verbal Self-Defense. New York: Doreset Press.
This book deals with skills needed to respond to all types of verbal attack. Different verbal modes discussed are tone of voice, alternative scripts, body language, and men/women verbal victims. This book has a lot of good information in it. It depends on what you need it for as to its value to you.

Flesch, Rudolf. How to Write, Speak and Think More Effectively. New York: Penguin Books, original copyright, 1946 - up to 1951.
Lots of good stuff but a bit dry.

*Gail A. Cassidy*

Fletcher, Leon. How to Speak Like a Pro. New York: Ballantine Books.
> Very well organized, easy to follow, informative book. Great "Checkpoints" at the end of each chapter.

Frank, Milo. How to get Your Point Across in 30 Seconds - or Less. New York: Pocket Books. Short, easy read. Good for learning how to "tighten" talks.

Glass, Lillian. Say It . . . Right. New York: Perigee Books.
> I believe Lillian's background is in speech correction. She has worked privately with stars, especially to overcome speech impediments and accents.

Glass, Lillian. Talk to Win. New York: Perigee Books.
> In this book, Lillian works on vocal image--pitch, resonance, pronunciation, accent, facial expression and gesture. She's very much into face and body language as it affects speaking.

Hoff, Ron. "I Can See You Naked": A Fearless Guide to Making Great Presentations. Missouri: Universal Press.
> Fun, funny, easy to read, informative. I thoroughly enjoyed reading this book.

Leeds, Dorothy. Power Speak. New York: Berkley Books.
> Leeds is a guru of sorts in the field of speaking. She has also written Smart Questions. This has excellent information about getting ready to be a powerful speaker, overcoming speaking faults, conquering trouble spots, and mastering the fine points of powerful speaking. It includes excellent checklists and assignments.

Lewis, David. The Secret Language of Success. BBS Publishing.

Loehr, Dr. James and Peter McLaughlin. Mentally Tough. NY: Evans & Co.
> This book has excellent information, and segments can be found throughout this course.

Mooney, William & Donald J. Noone. ASAP: The Fastest Way to Create a Memorable Speech. New York: Barron's Educational Series.
> Book addresses using speaker's props, organizing thoughts into clear ideas, grabbing audience's interest and keeping it, preparing a superb speech really fast. Good, not great.

Osgood, Charles. Osgood on Speaking: How to Think on Your Feet Without Falling on Your Face. New York: William Morrow.
> Brief, large print, elementary and good points for any speaker.

Persons, Hal. The How-To of Great Speaking. Austin: Black & Taylor.
> EXCELLENT! I've used this book as a teaching manual (before I wrote my own). It is light, easy-to-understand, has great illustrations, and covers everything you need to know.

Schloff, Laurie & Marcia Yudkin. Smart Speaking. New York: Plume.
> From back cover: "This fast, easy, problem-solving guide to communicating effectively in a multitude of situations is for formal and informal occasions, at home and at the office, on the

phone, at meetings, at parties, before large or small audiences, at interviews and more. . . . it offers easy-to-remember advice on more than 100 common communication problems. . .".

Simmons, Sylvia. How to Be the Life of the Podium. New York: AMACOM (division of American Management Association).

This is a great book for a person who is a speaker. It doesn't tell how to become one. It has great openers, closers and everything in between to keep them listening. Great stories that make a point without preaching. A must-have for the pro.

Peoples, David A. Presentations Plus. New York: John Wiley & Sons.

This is a very good book for presenters, a different emphasis than for speakers. It tells how to deal with problem people in a presentation, how to use presentation materials, how to organize, how to set up a room - lots of good stuff.

Persons, Hal. The How-to of Great Speaking: Stage Techniques to Tame Those Butterflies. Texas: Black & Taylor.

This is more good information on presentations, rather than speaking alone. It helps with organizing, writing, and rehearsing a winning presentation, cultivating and developing one's voice, and developing one's own natural speaking style. It also has invaluable practical skills on the physical part of setting up and delivering a presentation. I'd buy it again.

Sarnoff, Dorothy. Never Be Nervous Again. New York: Crown Publishers.

Dorothy is a true guru of speaking. She does have wonderful examples of success stories among the Hollywood and Broadway set, as she was an actress originally. Entertaining, but not overly informative.

Sarnoff, Dorothy. Speech Can Change Your Life. New York: Dell Publishing.

This book has more "meat" in it. She has information on making your voice, your speaking, and your conversation better. She also works on preparing and delivering the speech. This is a good book, but there are better ones available.

Schlof, Laurie and Marcia Yudkin. Smark Speaking. New York: Penguine.

This book covers strategies for those who mumble or ramble or talk too loud.

Simmons, Sylvia. How To Be the Life of the Podium. NY: Amacom.

Good resource for openers, closers plus 10-step method of organizing, writing, and editing your speech. Good to have. Lots of ideas.

Van Ekeren, Glenn. Speaker's Sourcebook II. New Jersey: Prentice Hall.

Quotes, stories, and anecdotes for every occasion. Entertaining. Lots of information, but I prefer Simmons, How to Be the Life of the Podium, although this is a great addition to a speaker's library.

Walters, Dottie & Lilly Walters. Speak and Grow Rich. New Jersey: Prentice Hall.

Contains techniques and shortcuts today's top speakers use to generate huge annual fees. Explains how to succeed at professional speaking--topics and titles that attract paid bookings; how to use PR, promotion, and advertising to obtain bookings; how to establish fees; how to overcome stage fright; how to handlehecklers; how to set up headquarters, sell programs to meeting planners. Tells advantages of working with speakers bureaus and agents, and how to boost profits with speaker products. Worth having if this a field you want to pursue.

Wilder, Lilyan. <u>Seven Steps to Fearless Speaking</u>. NY: John Wiley.Lessons on coping with panic, preparing your talk, and addressing special situations. Has stories to back up her points.

Woodall, Marian. <u>How to Think on Your Feet</u>. New York: Time Warner.

98-page paperback written by college professor with emphasis on thinking on your feet, dealing with questions, responding, and delivery. A different slant. Interesting.

# READY-TO-TEACH COURSES:

# Go to https://www.cassidycourses.com

Over twenty years ago, I became very concerned about the escalating numbers of bullying incident—kids hurting kids. Any form of rejection based on how someone looks or what their race, religion, or ethnic background is essentially a form of rejection that can turn into violence and can damage a child's self-esteem for years. According to authorities, two-thirds of school shootings are allegedly by teens who had been bullied. Bullied kids turn into angry adults who perpetuate their feelings through their own families, and the pattern continues.

How can that be stopped? To change someone's heart and beliefs has to start with the **experience** of acceptance and validation by one's own peers. I included the numerous testimonials in this book to give you an idea of how initially forced validation through having to find only positives in their peers turns into genuine admiration—what greater form of validation, of instilling the belief that *I'm okay!!*

*Speaking for Teens* is a half year course. Two additional quarter semester courses compliment this course beautifully. Below is how I've written about the two additional courses through the eyes of retired educator, Abby Foster.

### COURSE #2: "Discover Your Passion for Teens"

In the **Speaking for Teens** course, the Laws of Human Nature were addressed. The second part of what Abby determined to be needed for high school students is direction. *Discover Your Passion for Teens* is an 8-week elective, preferably for juniors. Every student is special, and this course zeros in on what makes each one special and how that knowledge can help them plan their futures.

Computerized aptitude tests are frequently used to determine careers in which students may be successful. *Discover Your Passion* takes a different approach. On a computerized test, a student must choose one answer, e.g. your favorite color. If their favorite color is not listed, the test is skewed, albeit ever so slightly.

With the exercises in *Discover Your Passion,* students are asked questions they can discuss with their peers, and there are never any wrong answers. These sessions are opportunities for insightful thinking for each student taking this elective.

Abby pondered a number of questions unrelated to her academic schedule. She thought, "Wouldn't it be nice if everyone could do what they wanted to do every day and still earn money? How great would it be to feel excited when you awaken every morning? Wouldn't everyone like to feel that what they do makes a difference in the world?"

Abby believes all of this is possible once a person knows what their passion is and knows how to put that passion to work. Master motivator and author, Barbara Sher, says it best in the title of her book, *I Would Do What I Love If Only I Knew What It Was.*

By the last session of this elective, Abby's experience is that students will know not only what their passion is but also how to earn money pursuing that passion whether it is full-time or as an income- producing hobby.

Abby recognizes that no two people are alike. Everyone has unique talents, knowledge, skills, and abilities. Finding which skill, which bit of knowledge, or which talent a person most enjoys using will lead to discovering their passion.

Two of Abby's favorite people concur. Wayne Dyer says, "There is no scarcity of opportunity to make a living at what you love; there's only a scarcity of resolve to make it happen. Even Oprah says, "Your job is to discover what your true calling is." Therein lies your happiness.

Abby developed *Discover Your Passion* as a course to help students discover their passion and earn money doing what they love. The four major objectives of this program are

(1) to help them clarify their passion,
(2) to prepare them for a job search or help some of the students to find their business,
(3) to familiarize them with marketing basics, and
(4) to help them learn how to make their dreams come true. Students can progress at their own rate or work in small groups.

She created major lesson divisions according to the information regarding the topic. Some sessions will take longer than others. Her experience is that students enjoy the journey, whether they are headed to college or to a vocational school to master a skill or to go out and find a job.

Abby designed the program to allow each participant to recognize what is special about themselves and to find a direction in life. The information students glean from their responses are important pieces necessary to complete their jigsaw passion puzzle. Fit them all together and they will have their passion.

## THE IMPORTANCE OF HAVING A PURPOSE

Another book that impacted Abby is *Man's Search for Meaning,* in which Victor Frankl tells of his horror-filled days as a prisoner in a Nazi prison camp. He said he made an interesting observation about those people who survived the terror and hardships of their ordeals.

He stated, in effect, that those who had a purpose in life survived; those who did not see any hope or believe they a purpose, died, even if physiologically equal. That is a significant observation.

Similarly, Wayne Dyer in *Real Magic* recalls the words of the prison inmate, "Nothing is more likely to help a person overcome or endure troubles than the consciousness of having a task in life."

Alter his words a bit by using the word *passion* in place of *task,* Abby read *"Nothing is more likely to help a person overcome or endure troubles than the consciousness of having a passion in life."* She believes that that is what teachers want students to uncover as they progress through this course.

**The #1 deadly fear of many people is having lived a meaningless life.** Abby's husband started his own business many years ago, because, as he said, he didn't want to wake up on his deathbed and say to himself, "I should have given it a shot."

> **"The only courage you ever need is the courage
> to live your heart's desire." -Oprah**

**Now is the time!!! This elective is the way!!!**

In her e-zine, Barbara Sher, author of *Wishcraft*, wrote "You're all obligated to do what you love because that's where your gifts lie and those gifts belong to all of us."

Implicit in that statement are **three premises**:
1) everyone is here for a purpose, and
2) everyone is here to help others, and
3) gravitating toward pleasure, e.g., doing what you love, is not only okay, it is mandatory if you want to help others and if you are seeking the wonderful illusives called happiness, satisfaction, and serenity.

That reminds Abby of her favorite quote **"The time to be happy is now; the place to be happy is here, and the way to be happy is by helping others."** - Charles Englehardt. That says it all.

Abby strongly believes that now that they are in high school, the time has come for students to discover how to use their gifts to make the world a better place. She believes that doing so will not only enrich their lives but also the lives of others. This is an opportunity to make the world a better place.

Having defined the baker's dozen of essential human nature laws, Abby got busy working on ways to implement what she felt was important to work on in order to motivate kids to learn and to be their best selves. She knew she couldn't just tell others to show respect to get respect, be non-judgmental, etc. **She needed a way for kids to experience these laws and hopefully adopt them.**

Over the next few years, Abby worked on the development of these three separate courses that would show rather than tell the laws of human nature with the intent of having them "buy in."

She started with Mindset or Belief and integrated the concepts into the three courses but devoted one course, **"Discover Your Passion for Teens,"** as the opportunity for teens to study themselves without judgment and make decisions based on what they experienced in the course.

The importance of belief! Napoleon Hill wrote in his book *Think and Grow Rich*: "What the mind can see and believe, it can achieve."

Abby believes the concept is still the same; it's still true -- if a student's mind can think up or conceive of an idea **and** believe in it, he can achieve it.

Abby continues: "If you believe you can do something, what's stopping you? What have you gotten to believe that acts as an obstacle to your success? Do you believe you can't "get" math, you can't make friends, you aren't bright, you can't sing, you are clumsy, etc." Some may be true, and that's fine. The point is, if you believe it, you act accordingly.

Abby recognizes that a person might **want** to be a singer, but if they can't carry a tune, they're not going to believe they can be a singer. Maybe they're horrible in math. If so, they're probably not going to WANT to be a scientist or an engineer, but they may be great in something else.

"If your mind can conceive and believe in doing something, you can achieve it. If you believe you can, what's stopping you? What have you gotten to believe that acts as an obstacle to your success?"

One of Abby's favorite sayings is from Henry Ford, the founder of Ford motors and the first assembly line for the manufacture of cars. He said, **"If you think you can**

**or you think you can't, you're right."** "If you think you can or if you think you can't, you're right."

To prove her point, Abby continued, "Belief applies not only to human beings, but also to the animal kingdom, even insects.

**EXAMPLE # 1:** If you catch flees and put them in a jar, they will jump up and hit their heads, jump up and hit their heads on the lid until finally they believe they can't get out. So, they sit on the bottom of the jar.

You can take the lid off of the jar, you can move the jar around, upside down, and the flees will not jump again. Why? Because they believe they can't get out. The point is: the flea comes to believe he cannot escape, even when the route to escape is clear; therefore, in his head, he cannot escape. That's how strong belief is.

**EXAMPLE #2:** Now, from a much larger point of view is that of an elephant. You may see a little elephant tied with a thin chain that goes around the elephant's leg attached to a stake in the ground, and well the elephant gets bigger and bigger and bigger, and finally there is this huge pachyderm who is tied to a stake in the ground with a little, thin chain. Obviously, he could just move it, pull his foot up, take it away; but he doesn't because—he believes he can't. He won't do what he can't believe he can do. This is the power of belief.

Like the elephants, many of us, especially kids, go through life hanging onto a belief that we cannot do something, simply because we failed at it once before.

**EXAMPLE #3:** Another example is Dr. Herbert Benson, a researcher from Harvard University. He was involved with a meditation movement way back when transcendental meditation became popular. Benson spent his career studying, among other things, meditation and the mind. He traveled to Tibet and observed how the mind can be trained as evidenced by the spiritual men and the monks could sit on a mountain top dressed in only a loincloth covered with a sheet and have the snow melt that fell onto the sheet.

From years of intense prayer and solitude, these monks were mentally capable of raising their body temperatures.

In some tribes, Dr. Benson found that the shaman or the medicine man could point to somebody after a trial and say, "Go home and die," and the person went home and died because he believed so strongly in the shaman—again, the power of belief!

If you think you can or you think you can't, you're right.

Frequently kids, especially "at risk" kids or kids who have been bullied believe they're incapable in some manner, who believe they're not accepted, who believe the teachers are being unfair to them. Some of their beliefs might be true, but they must be listened to and encouraged."

The point is," according to Abby, "our beliefs determine our success or lack of success in life. Kids need to know they are worthwhile, that they have something to offer the world. Everybody does, but sometimes talent is just not utilized because a person doesn't believe in the existence of that talent.

**Our beliefs guide us** as it does our students.

**ANOTHER EXAMPLE OF BELIEFS:** Sometimes beliefs have a tremendous effect on a person of any age. For two summers Abby had taught school administrators in Lithuania. This country had been under Russian rule for 50 years and had been subjected to a lot of destruction, including their educational system, especially where their schools were concerned. An American organization, A.P.P.L.E. (American Professional Partnership for Lithuanian Education) was founded and worked with teachers for 25 years before disbanding. American instructors worked with school teachers and administrators to teach them the latest ways that Americans do things in order to try to help them get their education system up to par.

They teachers had some beliefs that are different than what Abby was used to.

In the classrooms, there was no air-conditioning. On one hot day, Abby opened a window and opened the door to get a cross breeze. Immediately, one of the ladies got up and closed the window or closed the door. Abby then reopened the window and reopened the door, and they would say with fear in their voices, "No, no, you can't do that because if you sit in a draft, you'll get a cold and possibly die."

They believed what they said! They believed if they sat in a draft, they would die. Abby could not deny their wishes.

When Abby first got married, her mother-in-law was horrified that she washed my hair at night and went to bed. She believed Abby would die. She would get a cold and die. She believed that.

What beliefs do you, the reader, have about yourself, about your background? Are they positive or negative?

Abby always thought she couldn't go to college because "a nice Irish girl didn't run away from home" and "You're too big for your britches." That's what her father told her, but Abby changed her belief and started to believe she could go to college and pay for it herself, and she did.

What about your abilities? Do you believe you're good in math? Do you believe you're good in English? Do you believe you're good in science? Do you believe you're good in phys. ed.? Can you sing? Can you dance? What are your beliefs about yourself physically, mentally, spiritually? Those beliefs determine how you do in life.

And, of course, Abby believes the easy answer is: all you have to do is change those negative beliefs or have somebody point out to you what your strengths are. It's amazing when somebody hits the nail right on the head. You know it; they know it.

Every person has strengths and weaknesses. In this course, **Discover Your Passion for Teens,** Abby has exercises that enable each student to find theirs; and, along the way, may find their life's work. There are no wrong answers!

### COURSE #3: "Kids Mentoring Kids"

Abby was still concerned about the number of dropouts, mentally and/or physically, in the schools, especially schools in tougher areas.

Having taught in one capacity or another for decades, she finds her heart goes out to those kids who "fall between the cracks," the potential dropouts. It is for that reason that Abby developed the two programs already mentioned, both of which are enriching and fun. They are validating of each participant; they provide direction, and they teach communication skills, including human relations skills which translates immediately to improved civility among classmates.

Finally, it came to her: why not use the remaining quarter of the year, as an elective, to train kids to mentor other kids—juniors mentoring incoming freshmen.

**Abby's experience proved how one high school club (taught in 1/2 of one semester) and two electives can keep potential dropouts in school.**

As a result, Abby developed **Kids Mentoring Kids**, an elective for all juniors. She also developed a program which shows:

- How to set up a high school club that will provide acceptance, validation, and guidance to every child
- How to train club participants in listening skills and human relation skills
- How to improve college acceptance rates through participation in this club
- How to help every student discover their passion or purpose in life through a one-semester elective

- How to practice interviewing skills through this same elective
- How to improve speaking skills, self-confidence and esteem through a second one-semester elective.

A *Star Ledger* Editorial headline read: **Cause of death: Gangs!!!** "A study has found that more than half of all homicides in New Jersey are related to gang activity. . ."

Further in the editorial: "Law enforcement is only part of the solution. The best way to protect against the resulting violence is to understand the reasons young people are drawn to gangs . . . to find ways to counter that attraction."

Abby believes that an ideal "way to counter that attraction" is to start using mentoring in the high schools--juniors and seniors mentoring freshmen and sophomores or in lower grades where 8th graders mentor 4th graders. A club similar to the Key Club or Spanish Club or Poetry Club in high schools could be set up for the upper-class students where they would have an opportunity to not only discuss their underclass student challenges with the group but also master the basics of human nature and mentoring ethics that they can apply to all parts of their lives.

If every child were mentored as a freshman and then became a mentor, the world would indeed be a better place in which to live. Civility would be mainstream.

An administration complaint could be lack of time. It takes time to set up the appointment, get to the appointment, go there, return, etc. With this program, however, mentoring could be a part of the curriculum.

Abby found the mentoring experience to be a definite **win-win** **situation**. The person being mentored knows someone cares, someone is always there for them, merely a classroom or a phone call away, and someone can offer advice and guidance, someone older and wiser, even if it is only a couple of years.

On the other side of the coin, mentors have an opportunity to practice their listening skills and their human relation skills. They have an opportunity to be responsible for another person, which in turn makes them grow and become more self-sufficient.

The responsibility of having someone to mentor is something that cannot be taught; it can only be experienced.

What Abby learned from her diverse teaching opportunities is simple: **Everyone is special in some way, and when a person is able to recognize and act on that something special, that person and the world benefits.**

One of the best ways for high school kids to find what is special about themselves is to become a mentor. Abby developed this training to allow mentors to learn and know the tools to use to find what's special in others; however, it is the practice of using the tools with underclassmen that allows the significance of the tools to be internalized by the mentor.

They learn by doing. By putting their knowledge into practice while mentoring underclassmen, they "get" it!!

Abby believes that the secret of success for almost every person is to have someone in your corner (parent, friend, relative, priest, minister, teacher), rooting them on, cheering for them, helping them, validating them, and at times pointing out more effective ways to handle people and situations in life without tearing them down in the process.

## IMPRESSIVE STATISTICS:

- A research study provided these results on mentoring. "Children who met with a mentor three times a month for one year were 46 percent less likely to begin using illegal drugs, 27 percent decrease in initiating alcohol use, 37 percent decrease in lying to parents, 52 percent less likely to skip school, and 33 percent less likely to get into fights." (Statistics from a nationwide review of Big Brother/Big Sister's Programs by Tierney & Grossman)

- Why has mentoring grown into a social movement supported by government, schools, businesses and religious institutions alike? Because it works.

- Recognize that a mentor is a caring and concerned person. A mentor is a listener and a guide.

The value of mentoring is immeasurable! Take a look at the **STATISTICS,** keeping in mind that a large percentage of inmates are high school dropouts**.**

- Over 70,000 people will be released from state prison in New Jersey over the next five years. Check the number leaving your state's prisons.

- The average yearly cost of housing an inmate in New Jersey is $50,000. What is it in your state?

- The recidivism rate is over 60%. Two thirds of all prison releases end up back behind bars within three years.

- In 2004, a third of the 14,000 inmates who left state prison were let go with no obligation to hold a job, submit to drug tests or report to a parole officer.

- States spend an estimated $44 billion annually on prisons alone, not including the costs of arrest and prosecution, the damage to crime victims, or the impact on families and communities.

- A high percentage of dropouts end up in prison, costing the state approximately $50,000 a year per inmate. If 8 out of 10 potential dropouts stayed out of prison as a result of this program, there would be **savings of millions of dollars a year.** (The New Jersey Institute for Social Justice and the New Jersey Public Policy Research Institute's Re-Entry Roundtable report, June 20, 2003, Trenton, NJ. entitled "Community Re-Entry of Adolescents from N.J.'s Juvenile Justice System," by Bruce B. Stout, Ph.D., University of Medicine and Dentistry of NJ.)

- In the June 28, 2007, *Star Ledger,* an article from Washington, states "Prisons and jails added more than 42,000 inmates last year, the largest increase since 2000.

"Overall, the total number of people behind bars—including those held in local jails—was more than 2.2 million, according to the Justice Department's Bureau of Justice Statistics."

Abby believes that a formalized mentoring program in high schools could reduce these statistics by a quarter, a third, a half, or more. Any significant reduction would be accompanied by a corresponding reduction of costs to taxpayers. That would be a true win-win situation.

She wants teachers to remember, a mentor is someone who has a positive impact on the lives of others, someone who sees more talent, ability, and "specialness" within their mentoree, than the mentoree sees in herself, and someone who helps bring out these special traits and characteristics.

Abby points out that most people have had a mentor at some point in their lives. He or she may have come in the form of a teacher, a parent, a relative, an aunt, uncle, maybe a guardian, an older friend, a counselor, a coach, a minister, priest, rabbi, cleric, tutor, expert – somebody who believed in them, encouraged them to be the best they could be, and someone who had a positive influence on them. Not everyone, however, has been as fortunate, and it is for them that the mentor is here. The mentor now has an opportunity to impact their mentees' lives.

Abby read about actor, Denzel Washington, who believes that his success in life is due to a mentor he had as a teenager in an after-school boys' club. He was born and raised in a part of New York that was very tough, the streets were tough, gangs were prevalent. He lived in a bad section. And had he taken the wrong path, he certainly would not be the Denzel Washington everyone knows today who is famous and has done such a great job in the movies.

A couple of years ago, he wrote a book called, *A Hand to Guide Me*, which showcases how mentors have shaped the lives of people we all know and respect, from baseball legend Hank Aaron, Mohammed Ali, Bob Woodward – Bob Woodward who was a reporter during the Nixon time. He included people such as Yogi Berra, Danny Glover, the actor, Whoopi Goldberg, and over 60 other famous people. Every one of them had a mentor, somebody who believed in them and encouraged them.

As Abby frequently stated, "It's amazing how having somebody believe in you really makes you want to do the best that you can do. Sometimes parents or people who are close are just too busy surviving, earning a living; and that's where a mentor comes in. That is exactly what high school mentors will be doing – accepting and encouraging mentees to be the best that he or she can be. Young mentors now have an opportunity to impact their mentee's life."

Being a mentor means showing acceptance and guidance to someone who needs support, i.e., making a difference in someone's life. The reward for the mentor is the tremendous satisfaction awaiting as they watch their mentorees grow and develop into the people they desire to be.

The need for conscientious, sincere, caring, sensitive mentors is overwhelming. If administrators looked at the numbers of kids in trouble, they would have an idea of just how great the need for help is.

"*U.S. News & World Report* reported that, although conventional illiteracy – the inability to read a simple message in any language – had virtually disappeared in the United States, functional illiteracy – the inability to read and write at a level required to function in society – appeared to be increasing" (Myers, *Changing Our Minds, Negotiating English and Literacy*).

These functional illiterates and dropouts started out as unmotivated underachievers, mostly students who didn't fit in and could see no reason to stay in a place where they felt unaccepted and unappreciated, even if those conditions existed only in the student's mind.

Functional illiteracy and school dropouts are major contributors to the escalation of crime in communities, towns, and cities all over the United States. If mentoring can help lower the number of high school dropouts, it is a program well worth pursuing.

*Gail A. Cassidy*

Abby wondered, "Could mentoring reduce these statistics by a quarter, a third a half, or more? Any significant reduction would be accompanied by a corresponding reduction of costs to taxpayers. That would be a true win-win situation."

From Abby's experience, she believes that this program, in action, can prevent many potential dropouts from becoming a negative statistic. How? By simply enabling them to recognize not only their potential but also their positive effect on others.

*Success* means different things to different people. To Abby it means being of value to yourself, your family, and to society. It means being able to make a difference. It means liking yourself and believing in yourself.

Initially, Abby designed the mentoring programs for the students who needed help, whether academically or socially. To her great surprise, she found that those who benefitted most from the mentoring experience were the mentors.

Statements such as "I felt important," "It was the first time I felt looked up to," "I like the fact that I can be trusted and that I can help someone else," "I know that I need someone to talk to sometimes—being there for someone else is great," "I've learned that I can be a bigger person, a person to go to in a time of trouble," and "I loved helping the underclassmen" were typical of the responses she got on follow-up of the programs.

The responses from parents of those being mentored were also positive. One mother said told Abby that because of his mentor, her son actually looks forward to going to school. Before that, he was scared to leave his home. Teachers commented on improved grades of those being mentored. It's all good!

Abby believes we have to keep in mind one important question: What do gangs have to offer "disaffected" kids? They offer acceptance. She believes we can do better than that. She believes that Kids Mentoring Kids can promote acceptance/validation in a safe environment, in the schools.

How can that be done? Experiencing what it is like to help another person, to make a difference in the life of that person, is more impactful than words could relate. That is what this program is about.

Abby hopes other teachers will join her in the continuous adventure of learning. This is your, the reader's, opportunity to make a difference in the lives of your students.

> "One thing I know; the only ones among you who will be really happy are those who will have sought and found how to serve." – Albert Schweitzer

There are kids who are not at risk as well who could use a mentor to help them achieve their goals. This course shows them how.

Kids trained as mentors can have a positive impact on the lives of others. They can see more talent, ability, and "specialness" within their mentoree than those not paying attention can.

This course is designed to help teachers understand the mentoring process--what a mentor does and how he/she does it. Teachers will learn about the stories of students who have faced daunting challenges in their lives, and they will be introduced to the basic principles of how to best mentor those who are "at risk" for whatever reason.

Mentors will learn how to run a session, the rationale behind mentoring, the Mentor's code of Ethics, Advanced Mentoring Ideas, self-esteem/values, and interpersonal skills. Also included are motivational book summaries which give additional invaluable and timeless ideas.

This program was originally designed to help underclassmen adjust to high school, to gain confidence in themselves, and to have someone in the school they could rely on.

As previously stated, the evaluations came as a total surprise. The mentors were more frequently the benefactors. They said things such as, "I loved being a mentor because no one had ever looked up to me before. I felt important. I felt respected." You can't teach those things; you can only experience them. That's why **Kids Mentoring Kids** is so important to have in every school.

This program is self-explanatory and self-taught. In addition to the videos, there are transcripts of the videos, assignment sheets, handouts of all sorts, and materials to supplement every aspect of the course.

Abby had written the book, "The Validating Mentor" with the expectation that adults could mentor students. When she learned that it takes 6 months to clear someone interested in working with students—background check, fingerprinting, etc.—she chose to revise the material and encourage students to be mentors.

The concepts contained in this course work equally as well with friends, family, co-workers, or anyone who desires to improve his life and/or self-concept.

These are some of the kids who need your help. Many are high school dropouts or potential dropouts, young people who must learn to take 100% responsibility for all of their actions and who need your guidance to do so. These are the young adults who desire your help. Nobody gets through life without help. Everyone needs support and validation. Young people need help in every stage of their development.

Many of these "at risk" young adults may honestly wonder if they can change. "Assume a virtue, if you have it not" is the admonition Shakespeare would have given them.

Abby believes that students need to be encouraged to start acting as they desire to be, and they need to know they can be whatever they desire, one step at a time. The capacity for creating the life they want resides within each of them.

Being a mentor means showing acceptance and guidance to someone who needs your support. Your reward is the tremendous satisfaction awaiting you as you watch your mentorees grow and develop into the people they desire to be.

A mentor is a coach who seeks, finds, and points out the strengths of his mentoree. *Validation* implies recognition of someone's strengths.

A mentor is someone who has a positive impact on the lives of others, someone who sees more talent, ability, and "specialness" within their mentoree, than the mentoree sees in herself, and someone who helps bring out these special traits and characteristics.

As part of the training, Abby wants to make sure the mentor understands that the person being mentored, the mentoree, decides the direction, the speed, the route, the environment, the degree of intensity; and the mentor supports each step she takes.

The student mentor encourages the best direction, the appropriate speed, the best route, the cleanest environment, the safest coworkers, and the appropriate degree of intensity.

By the end of a year's mentoring, hopefully each mentoree will be able to successfully take her place and walk alone without the aid of a mentor.

Abby emphasizes that in order to maximize their potential, *mentorees first must feel they are safe, accepted, and respected as they are.* What helps to instill this feeling is constantly seeing the invisible tattoo on their foreheads, which reads, "Please make me feel important." In other words, "Don't criticize me or make me feel like a loser."

It is a mentor's job to help mentorees move through phase three, *Social-Acceptance* and phase four, *Self-Esteem*, in order to facilitate their reaching the highest level, Five, *Self-Actualization*. This final phase puts the mentoree in a position to make a difference in the world.

Abby emphasizes that feeling important is one of the deepest needs all human beings desire to have fulfilled. The words imply *acceptance*, and they imply *capability*, which is the basis of Level Three on the Hierarchy, *"Belongingness or Social Acceptance."*

*Everyone wants to be accepted,* either by their peers, family, church choir, motorcycle gang, colleagues, or whoever is important to them in their lives.

Once the feelings of acceptance occur, mentorees can reach toward the next Level, *"Esteem/Ego Status."* The Validating Mentor facilitates movement from one level to another, as can be seen in the *Mentoring Code of Ethics.*

Abby states that in one way or another, people young and old will gravitate toward someone who provides a source of validation. Validation is a human need, and this is where being a mentor comes into play. This is their opportunity to help mentorees experience acceptance and validation.

The fifth level of the Hierarchy is *Making a Difference.* With the help of mentors, mentorees will be at the point where they can make a difference--in their own lives and in the lives of those for whom they care.

Abby stressed it is important to remember that *positives do work.* If mentorees believe they can improve, they will. George Reeves, sixth grade teacher of Norman Vincent Peale told his special student, "You can if you think you can." And Peale proved his teacher right.

Overcoming years of negativity and poor results may be the greatest challenge for those who are unmotivated. While mentorees' improvement may not be vast, their improvement is possible by moving in small increments toward a higher level of proficiency in their job skills and their interpersonal skills.

Abby reminds mentors of the need to *show lively enthusiasm,* especially with an unmotivated mentoree. If the mentor shows no enthusiasm, the mentoree will reflect none. We "mirror" what we see, and this population is no exception to this rule. And if we don't feel it, again, as previously stated, take Shakespeare's advice, "Assume a virtue, if you have it not." Or, in the vernacular, "Fake it until you make it."

*It is human nature to desire fun or pleasure over pain.* Mentoring in an atmosphere of fun and/or pleasure enables young people to pay closer attention and retain direction better.

Abby's philosophy behind *The Validating Mentor* consists of five specific provisions:

(1) provides a **safe atmosphere**--physically and mentally (no insults, no making someone wrong, no demeaning comments),

(2) validates students through their efforts by **recognizing what they have done well** or done correctly,

(3) establishes **relevance**--something they can relate to--in their assignments, and

(4) **builds on their successes.** This philosophy of learning also

(5) introduces the element of **fun,** a guaranteed way to encourage learning and growth.

Under the appropriate conditions, validating mentoring can be the foundation for

(1) improved self-esteem and

(2) self-concept, and

(3) improved interpersonal skills.

These benefits are not so surprising if one looks closely at the concepts inherent in the principles of human nature.

Validating mentoring means taking a personal interest in a mentoree, supporting the paths she takes.

Validating mentoring means helping the mentoree strive toward his highest aspirations, not only in career choice but also in the pursuit of happiness in his life.

Validating mentors share their knowledge and experiences in the hope that their mentoree will reach a high level of achievement.

Validating mentors promote the importance of responsibility both at home and away from it.

Validating mentors care about the well-being of themselves and their families and model the behavior they want their mentorees to follow.

Validating mentors receive the greatest gift--satisfaction in knowing they have made a difference.

Charles Engelhardt said it best: "The time to be happy is now. The place to be happy is here, and the way to be happy is by helping others."

## WHAT ARE THE CAUSES OF THE PROBLEM?

According to Abby's research the causes of the problem relates to students' homes and socio-economic backgrounds, parents who are in the "survival" state and do not have adequate time for their children, the attraction of gang membership, the school's lack of effectiveness due to lack of resources, the lack of competence of some teachers are a few of the obvious reasons why students lose interest in school and end up dropping out.

Other students with similar backgrounds, however, frequently overcome these causes; therefore, society has an obligation to look further for remedies to vastly reduce these challenges.

What is the one thing that every human being wants? "Acceptance" by somebody or some group may be a good guess. "Acceptance" can also explain the popularity of gangs, people who accept one another.

One reason for dropping out of school could very well be the lack of success that students have encountered throughout their schooling. Lack of success frequently equates to lack of confidence and lack of self-esteem, two major roadblocks to successful learning experiences and, conversely, two motivators for getting into trouble.

When students have experienced continual failure throughout their schooling, by the time they are in high school, their course may seem to be set. Students' lack of motivation can be attributed partially to the fact that they had not done well in previous classes. As David Berliner argues, "If we foolishly structure schools so that many students are regularly bored, threatened, or punished in them, who would be so naive as to assume those students would thereafter love learning?" (Berliner 349).

Lastly, many of these students do not feel valued by their teachers. Why? One reason is they are on the track, which is perceived by many educators as *inferior*, therefore, the students must be the same.

The "tracked" kids are those who are always in trouble, the kids who don't care, the kids who have been tracked from their elementary years on through high school, in spite of studies which confirm the fact that tracking works to the disadvantage of most children (Berliner 207). Their opinions do not count.

Unfortunately, "students believe that tracking decisions reflect judgments about their personal abilities and prospects; thus, those decisions set up expectations in students that tend to become self-fulfilling prophecies. This means that ability and tracking systems repeatedly give most students the cruel and unfair message that they just don't measure up" (Berliner 322). This message has a definite adverse effect on self-esteem.

## WHAT ARE SOME SOLUTIONS?

*Gail A. Cassidy*

Many of the primary causes of poor performance in school (dislike of reading, boredom, irrelevance, lack of previous success, and tracking) can be addressed with a revitalized curriculum which enables students to experience success, but that is the responsibility of the local school districts and unfortunately out of the purview of the average citizen.

Mentors can address this need by having students first learn their strengths (we all have some) and aptitudes and then exposing them to the opportunities available to them. Our goal as mentors is to take them out of the "failure" category.

In an attempt to undo the negativity most "dropouts" experienced in school, mentors can encourage (but don't insist on) them to get their high school diplomas either through the country vocational school or their GED through the local colleges. This step, however, is not a requirement for continued mentoring.

Abby's one goal is to help students and young adults prepare themselves to be in the position to obtain well-paying jobs, not minimum wage opportunities. When students do what they enjoy doing, they are apt to be more productive and more successful. Contact with someone who cares is invaluable.

## TOP 15 BENEFITS OF WORKING WITH A MENTOR

1. Mentors are familiar with you, your background, your interests, and your goals.
2. Mentors can help you uncover old dreams and activities that made you feel special.
3. Mentors can help you to follow through on your life's purpose.
4. Mentors can help you stay motivated.
5. Mentors can help you find greater happiness in your life.
6. Mentors can help you learn how to complete your past.
7. Mentors can help you restore your energy.
8. Mentors can help you get your needs met.
9. Mentors can help you capitalize on your skills and abilities.
10. Mentors can help you live by your value system.
11. Mentors can help you eliminate things in your life that are not in your best interests.
12. Mentors can help you maintain an upbeat, positive attitude.
13. Mentors can help you handle difficult, challenging situations.
14. Mentors can help you develop a stronger community.
15. Mentors can help you be the best person you can be.

The way the mentor knows so much about those they are mentoring is because the mentor will help their mentoree complete the following forms:

- **PERSONAL CHALLENGES**, a one-page list of questions about what the mentoree wants out of life. This is good for the mentor to complete as well.

- **ASSESSMENT**. This is a two-page rating form which will help the mentoree figure out how he/she feels about their environment, personal well-being, mental well-being, relationships, vocation/career/finance areas of their life.

- **10 Goals to Reach in the Next 90 Days**, a page which helps the mentoree set goals for now and for the future.

Two additional pages – **SAMPLE SKILLS** and **CAUSES/ISSUES** will help the mentor and the mentoree zero in on what's important to each.

**The Weekly Preparation Form** will be used every week to in order for the mentoree to self-monitor his/her progress.

## THINGS TO TALK ABOUT

**How we feel about ourselves has an influence on how we live our lives and how we interact with others—our peers, teachers, family members, friends.**

Rather than directly asking, "How are you feeling about yourself?" you could ask, **"How do you feel about your classes, your classmates, your teachers."** Try to elicit specific instances of why they feel as they do.

For example, if they state that a teacher is picking on them in math class, ask them to tell you more about that. You may find that math is particularly challenging to them, and here is where you can suggest getting extra help or talking to their guidance counselor about help available.

You could ask, **"What do you want to do when you graduate?"** The answer to this question could give you the information you need to better understand how they are viewing their lives.

Attitudes toward their classmates, teachers, friends, and family will usually come through when they talk about their experiences in school. **Remember, your primary goals are 1) to keep them in school and 2) help them recognize what is special about themselves.**

*Gail A. Cassidy*

## CONCLUSION

Our kids are our future! We are currently living in a divided world today, a world afflicted by a killer virus that is keeping many of us in our homes. We have to ask ourselves, "How can be prepare our kids today to be the best that they can be and live a life of joy and meaning?" When we have answered that question, we will have solved a major challenge in today's society.

**Please join me in helping provide every high school student with what every human being desires: acceptance and validation!!**